...ORGANICliving

MICHAEL VAN STRATEN

••• photographs by **DAVID LOFTUS**

RODALE

This book is dedicated to my grandson Jamie, in the hope that he will inherit an ecologically better Earth than my generation has created for its children. It still is not too late to reverse the damage of global warming and environmental pollution and if this book helps to make people more aware of the simple changes that will make a difference, I shall be happy.

RODALE

WE INSPIRE AND ENABLE PEOPLE TO IMPROVE
THEIR LIVES AND THE WORLD AROUND THEM

Simultaneously published by Frances Lincoln Limited,
4 Torriano Mews, Torriano Avenue, London NW5 2RZ

Michael van Straten's Organic Living
First Frances Lincoln edition: 2001
Michael van Straten is hereby identified as the author of this work.

Design and typesetting by Caroline Hillier
Set in Wunderlich
Printed in Italy

Library of Congress Catalog No. 2001 000418
ISBN 0-87596-930-5

Distributed in the book trade by St. Martin's Press

2 4 6 8 10 9 7 5 3 1

contents

... introduction

This is a very personal book born out of my passionate concern for the health of the people on this planet and for the health of the planet itself. I first became aware of the word "organic" as a teenager growing up in the small country town of Tring, in Hertfordshire, England, where one of the most famous organic farms, Champneys, had been established by Stanley Lief. At that time Champneys was the mecca of natural healing, and Stanley Lief one of the great pioneers of alternative medicine.

As a teenager I visited Champneys regularly both as a friend of the Lief children and because a number of my parents' friends went there for treatment. In those days it was a place where very ill people went in desperation, and it was as far removed from the modern concept of plush health spas as you could possibly imagine. The regime was rigid: water treatments, exercises, massages, fasting, osteopathy, early morning walks, afternoon rests in total silence, evening lectures, no tea, coffee, or alcohol, no smoking, and a very strict vegetarian diet. The beautiful mansion house had wonderful grounds and

Appreciating the beauty of nature, both on the grand scale and in the graceful line and structure of a roadside weed, is part of an organic outlook on living.

an exquisitely maintained vegetable garden, which Stanley Lief ruled over, as he did his patients, with a rod of iron. No chemicals were allowed on the garden, no artificial sprays, not even the comparatively primitive insecticides and pesticides that were available in the mid-1950s. This was my introduction to organic gardening and the idea that food, environment, and health were inextricably tied together.

That was 45 years ago and my experiences at Champneys sowed the organic seeds in me, which resulted in my becoming a student at the British College of Naturopathy and Osteopathy in Hampstead, London. There, long before the hippie era of the 1960s, dandelion coffee, vegetarianism, and pure organic food was the rule, not the exception. Since 1964 the core of my practice as a naturopath and osteopath has been the interdependency of health and lifestyle, and the overwhelming importance of living as "green" a life as possible. That is why this book isn't just about organic food and the risks and dangers of a nonorganic lifestyle, but it's a book that encompasses the macrocosm of world green issues and the microcosm of the body's internal environment.

This book won't tell you how to turn your kitchen, your home, your office, industry, agriculture, and the world green in 10 easy lessons, but it will serve as an introduction to the many factors that impinge on people and the equally many ways people can impinge, for good or bad, on the rest of the world. I discuss the effects of pollution and the benefits of organic farming, and I include a wealth of practical, simple information on basic nutrition, the ways people's nutritional needs vary from age to age, and the contribution of organic food to better health. You'll also find information on natural beauty products and treatments, sample some stress-busting exercises, and learn about alternative natural therapies.

The book also explores the importance of recycling domestic waste and conserving energy in the home, as well as taking a look in the cabinet under your sink to see how you can green that dungeon of toxic and polluting chemicals. And when it comes to your home, there are so many ways you can reduce, reuse, and recycle. I share information on the use of recycled building materials, nontoxic paints, natural floor and wall

Living an organic lifestyle means not only looking after our bodies by eating organic food but also taking care of the environment in which we live.

coverings, and the use of environmentally friendly bricks, wood, and insulating materials.

If you're a gardener, or a gardener want-to-be, you'll be interested in the organic growing basics that you can use in your own backyard. Important aspects of organic gardening include good garden design and layout, as well as selecting plant species that have good natural resistance to pests and diseases. You'll find helpful information on these topics, plus essential maintenance techniques and instructions for building the all-important compost heap.

share *Organic Living* with a friend

There's not much point writing a book about green issues, the environment, and ecology if you cut down more trees to print it than it saves. So if you are reading this introduction, I hope you will buy the book and pass it around among your friends. After 35 years of treating patients and 25 years of running an alternative health phone-in program on London's major talk-radio station, I have learned how important it is to reach, not preach. And through this book I hope to reach as many people as possible and make them think about the world we live in. If you and everyone else who reads it recycle more household waste, add just one organic product a week to your shopping basket, and realize the significance of turning down your home thermostat a few degrees in winter, then it will have made a difference.

But beyond recycling and reducing consumption, there are health benefits, and not just a greener environment, cleaner air, and purer water. Avoiding chemical residues from the farming industry is a real plus for all of us. If you are considering having children, if you are pregnant or breastfeeding, or if you are feeding small children, the importance of organic food cannot be overestimated. And it is worth noting that organic food is not just food grown without chemicals. Certified organic food products must also be free of the artificial colorings, preservatives, flavorings,

sweeteners, and other additives that may trigger behavioral problems and allergic reactions in small children.

If you run a business or industry, you are in a position to make an enormous contribution to the greening of our world. You can specify that recycled products be used in your business, you can insist on recycling of all your company's waste, and you can buy green energy for your factory, warehouse, or office. You can even stipulate that organic food be served in your staff cafeteria.

Unfortunately, despite the huge growing awareness of all these green issues, most governments pay no more than lip service to the principles involved. Most governments have only two basic desires—to stay in power, and to make friends with big business—and the first is entirely dependent on the second. For this reason, reducing industrial emissions to levels that will help reduce global warming are ignored or traded off with emerging countries who need the cash and probably don't control their own emissions anyway. Highly toxic crop sprays, which Western countries ban on their own farms, are still manufactured and exported to third-world countries where there is little control over their use. What's more, the effects on workers in industries like cotton, cocoa, coffee, and tea production are out of sight, out of mind.

going organic

It seems extraordinary to me that governments appoint officials responsible for the environment, yet fail to provide them with legal or financial support to enact and enforce more green legislation. If it weren't for the pressure put on governments worldwide by organizations like Friends of the Earth, Greenpeace, and the World Wide Fund for Nature, none of them would ever have moved an inch toward greener legislation. It's only because of the growing anxiety among ordinary people about the damage being done to our planet, and the potential harm to our children's health, that meaningful changes will ever take place.

A major question is whether the economics of "going organic" can ever stack up against conventional farming, food production, construction, and energy needs. The answer is definitely yes. All major industries cry ruin and bankruptcy at the prospect of being forced to change the way they do things. Automobile manufacturers fought against catalytic converters and lead-free gasoline for years, at first saying it wasn't possible, then saying it would never be financially viable. Finally, when they were forced to do it, there didn't seem to be real problems at all. On the other side of the coin, companies wanting to introduce highly profitable new technologies claim, as they have with genetically modified (GM) foods, that it's the only way to feed the Third World, that they can dramatically increase yields and reduce crop losses to disease and pests.

the problems with GM foods

In truth, what the GM companies are after is market domination. A few years ago none of the five major agrochemical companies was involved in the seed industry; now they dominate it. And by building what is referred to as terminator genes into their seeds, they are attempting to ensure that each batch of seed will produce one crop only, and the seed from that crop will be sterile. What is more, sales of the seed simultaneously increase sales of the pesticides or herbicides that it is designed to withstand. Farmers will no longer be able to follow the ancient practice of saving their seed corn for the next year's crop—they will have to buy it from one of the "big five." Farmers in emerging countries will not be able to afford the new "more productive" seed or the chemicals that go with it. Talk of saving the Third World from starvation is pious propaganda.

The vast multinational food companies that incorporate GM foods into their products also adopt policies that they think they can get away with. Two major food producers in the United States admit that some of their products contain genetically modified materials, but American citizens can't possibly tell which because the companies refuse to state on their labels whether or not products are GM free.

In Great Britain, where consumers have been much more active and forced retailers to abandon GM foods, these same companies are removing all genetically modified ingredients from their products. Since about 33 percent of the U.S. corn crop grown in 1999 was genetically engineered, what are your chances of buying any corn-based product—including corn starch and corn syrup—that is free from this material?

The U.S. Food and Drug Administration (FDA) has consistently refused to require safety testing of genetically engineered ingredients or require their labeling before they are allowed to go on to the market. But the FDA has enforced major recalls of taco shell products that were found to be contaminated by a genetically modified corn called 'StarLink'. This corn, licensed for animal feed only and potentially a cause of human allergic reactions, has found its way into two major brands.

The food, energy, and petrochemical industries won't give up without a fight. Certainly in Great Britain there have been enormous and tragic government blunders regarding food safety and the intensive farming industry. The scandal over salmonella in eggs and indeed in the whole chicken flock in Britain; the lies and deceit surrounding bovine spongiform encephalopathy (BSE, or mad cow disease) and its human form, Creutzfeldt-Jakob disease (CJD); and the spectacle of a government minister publicly feeding a hamburger to his daughter as a "photo opportunity" just to prove that British beef was safe—it's hard to even think about these. In fact, the British government instituted a large fund to compensate families who have been affected by the dreadful illness CJD.

In spite of leading academics pointing to the risk of BSE jumping species to humans, nobody listened because the financial implications and the effect on the interests of multinational corporations was too vast to contemplate. The thousands of potential deaths are far more awful. Yet there hasn't been a single case of BSE in cattle bred from wholly organic cattle on an organic farm in Britain. Is there a lesson to be learned here?

The more I work in the field of human health and the more I learn about the human body, the more I realize how slender a thread life hangs on. But people are incredibly adaptable. We survive in the deepest frozen wastes on a diet of seal blubber, in the arid deserts of the Kalahari on roots and shoots and the occasional animal, and in the steamy, humid rainforests of Brazil on fish, grains, and tropical fruits. Some people live below sea level at the Dead Sea and in the thin air of Tibetan mountain villages. We cope with famine, drought, feast, and plenty because the human body has this almost magical property of homeostasis. This innate ability to maintain the physiological and chemical balances within the body, in spite of external and internal influences, is the reason for our survival.

But there is a point at which even this ability fails us and we cannot survive. I also believe our planet and its global environment also have the ability of homeostasis and the power to adapt to changing circumstances. But just as for people, homeostasis for the planet has finite limits, and we exceed them at our peril. The chemical pollution of our atmosphere, of the air we breathe, the water we drink, the seas we fish, and the soil that produces our food puts us at peril. And if you find that alarming, I'm glad, because until people are alarmed they won't act. As a species, we are great at shutting the stable door after the horse has bolted. In global terms, the horse is only just sticking his nose out, and the more people that act now, in however small a way, the greater our chances of shutting the door before it's too late.

Of course we have to balance risks and benefits, and we have to practice a little genuine risk assessment. After all, you are more likely to die of a heart attack than of pesticide poisoning, and your child is much more likely to get sick through not eating any fruit and vegetables than from injesting chemical residues on nonorganic ones. It's also true that many so-called safety measures have little effect in the long term. Putting speed bumps in residential areas may slow down the traffic and reduce the risk of accidents, but as the endless streams of cars and trucks brake for the bump and then accelerate up to the next one, the level of exhaust fume pollution rises dramatically. So which is more hazardous?

In all countries where seat belts have become mandatory, there is no evidence of a reduction in accidents. Statistics show that when you're wearing a seat belt you feel safer, so you drive faster and brake later. But industry has never done a similar type of in-depth risk assessment of the thousands of chemicals that we are exposed to on a daily basis. It is hard to prove that anything is totally safe, but it is disgraceful to use this as an excuse for not putting the burden of proof on manufacturers of patently toxic materials before they are used in even tiny concentrations in hazardous situations—situations that affect our planet, that damage wildlife, and that can directly affect the health of adults, their children, and their children's children.

We should have learned a painful and tragic lesson from the thalidomide disaster in the 1950s, but we haven't. A generation later, it now appears that the children of thalidomide children may be suffering congenital deformities, too. How long will it be before we acknowledge that Gulf War syndrome is the result of chemical exposure to substances very similar to some of the worst of the agricultural chemicals? It is terrifying to think about.

No one can entirely change the way they live overnight, but in the words of Mao Tse-tung, "A march of a thousand miles starts with one step."

Wildflowers once grew in great abundance. If each of us can learn to take better care of our environment, the meadows may bloom again.

... the natural environment

While it may be impossible in the modern world to live a completely organic lifestyle—where all the products you use and all the food you eat are either manufactured or grown without synthetic chemicals and without harming the earth—every person who takes a step toward organic living makes a difference. Every family that encourages a household culture of organic living makes an even greater difference by educating their children to live organically in the future. Every tiny saving of fuel and every purchase of organically grown food will help. Each of these small steps contributes to a reduction of toxic material in our environment and a lower rate of global warming.

As the worldwide consumption of fossil fuels increases year after year, so does atmospheric pollution and the production of greenhouse gases (particularly carbon dioxide). The result is global warming and significant climate changes. Melting ice caps, rising sea levels, coastal flooding, and other climatic disasters are only some of the consequences of our exorbitant use of fuel resources.

Olive trees thrive in poor soil and on inaccessible hillsides, and the traditional methods that are still used in their cultivation do not damage the environment.

A major factor in this equation is the amount of energy used by conventional farming. Huge amounts of fossil fuels are used to manufacture synthetic fertilizers, pesticides, fungicides, herbicides, and other agrochemicals, as well as to transport the raw materials and finished products and apply them to the land. The amount of fossil fuel used in crop production is estimated at 2.2 percent of total energy usage in the United States. Adopting organic farming systems on an international scale would lead to substantial savings in fuel costs. More importantly, it would make a major contribution to the reduction of greenhouse gases in the atmosphere.

Over the last 20 years, the efforts of activist groups like Friends of the Earth as well as massive media coverage of environmental disasters caused by pollution, nuclear and chemical accidents, acid rain, and toxic waste have made us all more aware of how much we waste our planet's resources and pollute the natural environment—and a great deal of that waste and contamination can be attributed to the modern conventional farm.

farming and the environment

Organic farming is seen by many as necessary to the future of life on earth, yet it is barely 100 years since all agriculture was essentially organic. Until the 19th-century German chemist Baron Justus von Liebig invented an artificial chemical fertilizer, most fields and farms were fertilized with manure from their own livestock or with plant refuse—gigantic sources of compost that were entirely organic. Once von Liebig found a way of producing artificial fertilizer, this natural cycle was broken.

The new fertilizer must have seemed miraculous to farmers, who were under constant pressure to produce more food, and when World War II broke out, undermanned farms took grateful advantage of every available chemical aid. These included the pesticide DDT, which was originally developed by the military to kill mosquitoes, lice, and fleas, and the organophosphate compounds, which were intended for use as nerve gases. Agricultural use of pesticides increased dramatically in the post-war years, and a cycle of dependency was created: Insects developed resistance to the chemicals, which meant chemicals had to be used more frequently in order to have any affect. At the same time, fertilizers were being poured onto fields that were continuously cropped, giving the soil no opportunity to replenish its natural minerals, so that it, too, needed larger doses of chemicals to support plant growth.

Today, nearly 4 million tons of agrochemicals are used annually in the United States alone—which is about 30 times the amount used in 1945—and hundreds of pesticides are licensed for use around the world. Not all of them are harmful, but many have troubling side effects. In humans, dangers linked to agrochemicals include birth defects, damage to reproductive systems, interference with hormone systems, brain or nervous system damage, damage to immune systems, and a greater risk of developing certain cancers. As an example, the preliminary results of a recent study at Stanford University's School of Medicine show that people who use pesticides in their home and garden have an increased risk of developing Parkinson's Disease.

Despite all the warnings and adverse publicity, the worldwide use of nonagricultural pesticides is growing dramatically. According to *World Crop Protection News,* the global market for nonagricultural pesticides is worth about $7 billion per year and is growing by 4 percent annually. The report also states that at least 12 percent of worldwide pesticides sales are nonagricultural. These highly toxic chemicals are used as fly and insect killers in the home, for the treatment of wood, or applied to golf courses and community areas. A staggering 40 percent of all household pesticides (with a value of more than $1 billion) are used in the United States.

In some countries, including India, airline passengers are sprayed with pesticides on arrival before being allowed off the aircraft. And planes flying to Australia, New Zealand, and the West Indies are routinely sprayed with long-acting insecticides before passengers board. There have been many reports of people suffering side effects from these chemicals.

According to one British study, pesticide use worldwide accounts for 14 percent of all known occupational injuries and 10 percent of all known fatalities. Most deaths from pesticide use occur in developing countries, many of which are still using chemicals that have been banned in Western countries. In 1999, for instance, the small West African country of Benin, whose economy relies heavily on agriculturally based industry, reported 60 documented deaths from exposure to farm chemicals.

Pesticides also have a serious impact on the biodiversity of the environment. Used on farms as pest controls, they can kill beneficial insects or plants as well as the target pest,

The agrochemical industry is one of the major contributors to the pollution of the atmosphere by greenhouse gas emissions.

thereby disrupting the natural balance of the farm's ecosystem and that of the surrounding countryside. Populations of insect-eating birds such as tits and wrens, which devour caterpillars and aphids, and blackbirds, thrushes, and starlings, which feed on crane flies and slugs, may decline as they lose their source of food, and birds may also die as a direct result of eating insects that have absorbed pesticides. The loss of birds deprives the farmer of useful pest-eating allies, and birds' predators suffer, too.

Without insect-eating birds around, a secondary pest may replace the primary one that was the original target of the pesticide. In addition, the primary pests may develop resistance to the pesticide, and different pesticides will be needed to control them. It is easy to see that using pesticides can be as inefficient as it is ecologically destructive.

Sadly, the destruction caused by agrochemicals is long-term, for many chemicals don't break down easily in the environment. In addition, pesticides drift when sprayed (it's been estimated that only 10 to 15 percent of a given pesticide will actually reach its target pest; the rest falls on hedges or woodland and can drift up to a mile in the wind), and the nitrates in fertilizers wash out of the fields into rivers and lakes, contaminating the water and the habitat.

Once chemical pesticide use was in full swing, it didn't take long for their negative effects to become apparent. In the 1950s, colonies of bald eagles in Florida began dying out because their weakened eggshells broke before their chicks could mature. Otters began to disappear from England's rivers. And, after a huge DDT spraying of a Douglas fir forest for spider mites, the trees died while the worst infestation of spider mites that had ever been seen in the area descended on crops. These were all signs that agrochemicals were destroying fragile ecosystems and spreading through the complex chains of life, leading, ultimately, to human beings.

farming and food

Water companies spend billions of dollars and use tremendous energy resources to filter pesticides and fertilizers out of drinking water. But water isn't the only source of pollution that could have negative effects on our health. There's no longer any doubt that the chemicals farmers apply to their crops and animals are found in our food.

The nonprofit organization Environmental Working Group has drawn on the results of U.S. government tests to show exactly which pesticides may be present in American

foods (find out on its Web site, www.foodnews.org). Pick up a shopping basket in the virtual supermarket and find out exactly what you may be exposed to and learn ways to reduce your intake of pesticides. (I bought pears, a loaf of whole-wheat bread, eggs, bacon, asparagus, and onions, and found I had 15 pesticide residues in my bag, including two carcinogens.) The average American apple contains four pesticide residues; those from other countries may be even worse. The group will also calculate how a child would fare after ingesting these pesticide residues.

(continued on page 22)

left and above: *Pesticides used on crops upset the balance of nature by destroying habitats and killing beneficial wildlife as well as pests.*

following pages: *Permanent flooding of low-lying coastal areas is one effect of global warming, as polar ice melts and sea levels rise.*

Cotton is one of the world's most heavily sprayed crops, but few people realize how much cottonseed oil is used to make margarine and many other processed foods. What's more, the chemical pollutants move through the food chain when the seedcake left behind after oil extraction is added to animal food. The main recipients are cattle used for beef and milk production. Of course, dairy products like cheese, cream, yogurt, and butter will also contain those chemicals.

Another source of serious concern is the antibiotics that were first introduced into farming just after World War II and that are now often used almost indiscriminately to treat livestock. Flocks of chickens, for instance, are rarely treated individually. For efficiency, antibiotics to treat or prevent bacterial infections are dispensed to the entire flock, whether they need them or not. Pigs, which are particularly prone to illness when reared in confined spaces, may be prescribed as many as 10 different antibiotics. Cows are regularly treated with antibiotics, sometimes as a preventive measure for mastitis (inflammation of the udder)—again, whether or not they're suffering from it. Fish farms are also big consumers of antibiotics, even though most of the treatment simply escapes into the environment.

While the British government has now banned four of the most widely used antibiotics, several of these are still in use in the United States. Like pesticide residues, they are filtering up the food chain and traces of growth hormones and antibiotics have been found in American dairy products.

One effect of the overuse of antibiotics in farming is that it has fostered the growth of "super-bacteria." Humans and animals have their own bacterial systems that help the body resist infection, so eating food containing super-bacteria—those already resistant to antibiotics—may make the host species less able to resist illnesses and less able to respond to any antibiotics doctors or vets use to treat them.

The message of unsafe farming practices has been underlined by a series of worrying food scares. The causes of the bovine spongiform encephalopathy (BSE)—commonly known as mad cow disease—outbreak in Great Britain have yet to be entirely explained, but unhealthy practices such as feeding the carcasses of animals to their same species and the low resistance to illness of herds raised in overcrowded conditions most likely have contributed to the problem.

The most recent worry is about genetically modified organisms (GMOs), which have come to the public's attention only during the last decade. Some scientists claim that genetically modified crops (also known as genetically engineered or GE crops) will benefit mankind by making plants hardier and less susceptible to pests and diseases, but the effects may be different in practice. The development of herbicide-resistant GM crops is likely to lead to an increase in the use of synthetic herbicides, for example.

Many genetically modified crops are already in general use. About one-third of the total production of soybeans in the United States is already genetically modified. One random genetic fingerprinting found that 2 in every 15 products on grocery store shelves may contain traces of GMOs. Because the long-term effects of GMOs on humans, animals, and the environment in general are not yet known, the news that governments had allowed GMOs to be used freely caused widespread alarm in the late 1990s, particularly in Europe. That concern spread to the United States in September 2000 when the Food and Drug Administration (FDA) confirmed the presence of illegal genetically modified corn in Taco Bell taco shells. The contaminating ingredient was 'StarLink', a variety genetically engineered to contain a plant pesticide that is approved for use in animal feed only. Many U.S. consumer groups are now calling for a ban on GM ingredients unless they are properly labeled and tested for safety—a practice that is currently voluntary.

Modern conventional agriculture relies heavily on large machinery to cultivate farmland and harvest crops, adding to the atmospheric pollution caused by burning fossil fuels.

While GMOs may eventually turn out to be as good for society as has been promised, they need to be fully understood before they can be used as safe sources of food. Until more is known about GMOs, planting experimental crops in areas where the wind allows their pollen to contaminate neighboring crops is clearly unwise, yet this practice is allowed in the United States.

As large companies, including the McDonald's fast-food chain, respond to consumer demand by refusing to accept GMOs in their products, it is clear that GMOs have a long way to go before the public considers them completely safe. Currently, all the leading supermarkets in Great Britain and others in Europe have banned selling products containing GM food. It's interesting to note that at least five U.S. supermarket chains are owned by European companies. Perhaps they will follow the no-GMO principle established for their European customers by not allowing GMOs in products sold in their American stores.

the organic farm

"Feed the soil, not the plants" is the founding principle of organic farming. This same concept applies to raising animals: Rather than relying on drugs and medicines, raise animals in a healthy environment. Instead of genetically modifying good plant strains or polluting fields, rivers, and wildlife with chemical fertilizers and pesticides, make the earth strong in itself. Feed the soil and you feed everything that comes out of it. Ultimately, you feed human beings.

Conventional farming systems do not necessarily conserve resources or return anything to the earth. By neglecting the structure of the soil and becoming reliant on pesticides and fertilizers, conventional farming methods treat the earth as something from which we can take without having to give anything back. As Englishman Albert Howard, the father of organic farming, said, it is "expecting altogether too much of the vegetable system that it should work only in this crude, brutal way . . . the apparent submission of nature has turned out only to be a great refusal to have so childish a manipulation imposed upon her."

Albert Howard was a young Englishman who was appointed Imperial Chemical Botanist at an experimental agricultural station in India in 1905. His work and observations there formed the basis of the organic movement. Over the next 40 years, he learned "how to grow healthy crops practically free from disease without any help from mycologists, entomologists, bacteriologists, agricultural chemists, statisticians, clearinghouses of information, artificial manures, spraying machines, insecticides, fungicides, germicides, and all the expensive paraphernalia of the modern experimental station."

One of the most important people influenced by Howard's work was J. I. Rodale, an eccentric U.S. electrical manufacturer who also did some farming, writing, and publishing. He struck up a correspondence with Albert Howard that eventually led to the magazine *Organic Farming and Gardening*, which still thrives but is now known simply as Rodale's *Organic Gardening*. His children and grandchildren have carried on the organic tradition, and today the Rodale Institute is known as the forerunner of organic gardening in the United States.

Another pioneer of organic farming was Lady Eve Balfour, who began applying Howard's methods on her farm in Suffolk, England, and chronicled her results in *The Living Soil*. The phenomenal response to her book was one of the forces behind the foundation in 1946 of the organization now known as the Soil Association, the leading proponent of organic standards in Great Britain.

From the outset, its founders were concerned about the health implications of the increasingly intensive agricultural

Wild grasses growing naturally on the outskirts of an organic farm create a friendly environment for a wide range of wildlife.

systems that were becoming commonplace after World War II, and the Soil Association (now a registered charity) is at the center of the campaign for safe, healthy food, an unpolluted countryside, and a sustainable farming policy—both in Britain and worldwide. It also certifies about 80 percent of Great Britain's organic foods.

In the United States, until quite recently each state was left to develop its own organic standards, making it hard for farmers to sell their organic produce abroad. With so many different governing bodies, it was hard for foreign countries to keep up with the varying standards used by different states. At the end of 2000, however, the U.S. Department of Agriculture (USDA) adopted nationwide organic standards, which undoubtedly make it easier for everyone buying organic products—importers and consumers alike—to know what they're getting.

Whatever country a farmer lives in, in short, "organic" refers to an agricultural system that encompasses:

★ Management practices that sustain soil health and fertility. Farmers build natural soil nutrients by planting cover crops so they don't need to rely on synthetic fertilizers.

★ The use of natural methods of pest, disease, and weed control. Weeds, insects, and other pests are managed without chemicals, but with earth-friendly methods such as beneficial insects and mechanical controls instead.

★ High standards of animal welfare. Animals are raised humanely, without using synthetic hormones or antibiotics, and they are raised on organic feed.

A conventional farmer who decides to switch to organic methods agrees to abide by a set of standards that govern all aspects of farming practice. The health of the soil lies at the heart of organic farming and is maintained using natural methods that do not strip the minerals from the soil or contaminate the crops or the environment. The use of

Pigs reared organically are allowed to live in the open air, following their natural patterns of behavior.

artificial fertilizers is prohibited. Pesticide usage is minimal and restricted, both in choice of product and application.

Crop rotation is the key technique in growing organic crops. Rather than repeatedly planting the same crop in the same place, crops and grazing for animals are rotated so nutrients used by the previous crop can be replenished. For example, an organic farmer will plant clover to replace the nitrogen used by the previous year's wheat crop; the clover can then be cut and used as mulch or harvested for compost, thus providing a double benefit. The choice of crop is also part of natural pest control. By planting a mosaic of crop habitats—grasses and vegetables, for example—the farmer provides a natural balance between pests and pest predators.

An organic farmer works in what is known as a "closed cycle." This means that the soil is fertilized with manure that has come from livestock reared on the farm, and animals are fed as much as possible on crops grown organically on the farm. In other words, what comes out of the earth is returned back to it. Animals are an integral part of most organic farms, and their welfare is paramount. This means raising them in humane and healthy conditions so that they develop their own natural immunities to disease, and avoiding reliance on antibiotics and other drugs. The farmer must also give his animals a dignified life and, as much as possible, a painless and stress-free death.

Taking on such a burden of responsibility is a major commitment. Even those who have their doubts about the benefits of organic food accept that an organic farm is a healthier environment than an industrial one. But there is no denying that farming organically is demanding.

Anywhere in the world, the process of going organic requires a conversion period. For the farmer, this means that herbicides are not allowed and the use of synthetic chemicals is severely restricted. The conversion period will take 2 years for most crops and 3 years for some, during which time the farmer's expenses are high and income is low. In order to be classified as organic, animals must be born on organic land to parents that have been managed to organic standards prior to their birth. Livestock management is changed to free-range systems and non-reliance on antibiotics, wormers, and other treatments. So it takes time, money, and effort to convert to farming organically.

The farmer who chooses to convert faces a difficult path in the initial stages, but that's where you come into the picture. Buy all your fresh fruit, vegetables, and meat from local organic producers wherever possible. If there is an organic farm nearby with a farm shop, a local organic farmers' market, or a local store that is selling genuine, local organic produce, make it the first stop on your shopping trip. Tell your friends and perhaps organize a bulk shopping program. Put pressure on your local supermarket to buy organic produce from local suppliers. This not only ensures the farmers' survival and success but reduces fuel consumption by bringing in supplies from local farms rather than from hundreds or even thousands of miles away.

The hard work continues once the farm has been certified as organic. Organic farms tend to be more labor-intensive. On a conventional nonorganic farm, for example, weeds can be controlled with herbicides and pests with pesticides. On an organic farm, weed and pest control has to be done by hand or mechanically rather than with a chemical spray. Happily, pests become less of a problem than on conventional farms as the farm's biodiversity is restored.

Organic animal care is similarly demanding. The health care of a flock or herd on an industrial farm usually consists of giving routine doses of antibiotics to prevent infection. This treatment is simply not allowed on an organic farm. The aim, in the first place, is to raise animals that are healthy enough to avoid illness, and in the second place, to avoid exposing them to unnecessary antibiotics. In the organic system, an animal's welfare is regarded as being vital to its health. This means that animals on an organic farm are—

under good, stringent certifications—given enough room to move freely, adequate natural ventilation and lighting, and proper bedding. Their food must be largely organic and must not include animal by-products, sawdust, or genetically modified ingredients. Up to 10 percent of the feed can be nonorganic, but this of course excludes chemicals of any sort. When it comes to their slaughter, live animals must be transported humanely, local slaughterhouses must be used wherever possible to avoid too much stress from traveling and, most compassionately, the animals must not be able to see the stunning and slaughter process while they wait.

As for the fields, a proportion of them are cropped, with the remainder growing regenerative plants such as clover or mustard to rebuild soil structure and replenish the nutrients that were used by the last crop. Before the next crop is sown, these regeneration plants, known as "green manure," are plowed back into the soil, where they supply natural sources of nitrogen and other nutrients for the next round of crops. Then the whole cycle begins again.

Organic farming involves having respect for the land and livestock, taking responsibility, and working hard. But there is a real satisfacton for farmers in knowing that they are working in harmony with the ecosystem and encouraging biodiversity of plants and wildlife. They are producing food that is free from toxic substances that might present a health hazard to themselves and their families as well as the final consumer. And farmers can sell their produce directly to consumers who understand what they are trying to do and appreciate the quality and taste of organic food. But it takes us as consumers to be willing to support organic farmers in order to complete the cycle and make the system successful. We'll benefit the farmers, the environment, and the health of our families.

The return to traditional mixed farming, in which animals play a central role, is one of the great pleasures and satisfactions for many organic farmers.

... we are what we eat

There is a huge and growing interest in eating more of the foods that nourish and protect the mind, body, and soul. However, while many of us want to eat healthily, we don't always know the best way to go about it. We may buy low-sugar foods with a high salt content or low-fat foods that are high in sugar in the mistaken belief that we are making healthy choices. We buy salami and sausage instead of a fattier-looking—but in fact less fatty—joint of meat. All of which means that the first rule in the search for healthier food is what you see is not always what you get—or want.

One of the first steps on the path to a healthy world and a healthy you is choosing organic food: It is the cornerstone of organic living. Organic food is better for the planet, better for the farmer and his livestock, and almost certainly better for you, too. The basis of good nutrition is eating a varied and balanced diet with plenty of fruit, vegetables, and whole grains. But by choosing organic foods, you get the extra benefit of avoiding the added colorings, flavorings,

Feeding our children organic food is particularly important because their nervous and immune systems are more vulnerable to damage while they are still developing.

preservatives, antioxidants, emulsifiers, stabilizers, and artificial sweeteners that are found in processed foods, as well as the residues of agricultural pesticides, hormones, and antibiotics. As an added bonus, you may even be consuming higher levels of nutrients.

As yet, the scientific evidence to support the theory that organic produce contains higher nutritional value than conventionally grown produce is unclear, but it seems to me a matter of common sense that food grown in rich, naturally fertilized soil will offer the optimum levels of vitamins, minerals, trace elements, and the beneficial phytonutrients (plant nutrients) that help to protect us against heart disease and cancer.

Whether or not organic produce contains more nutrients, the benefits of not ingesting unwanted chemicals are clear. And it has never been easier to buy organic produce—many supermarkets stock it, and there are dedicated organic food stores, home delivery services, and organic mail-order companies. You can even buy organic foods on the Internet. Personally, I find that organic fruits and vegetables simply taste a whole lot better. Once you have tried them there will be no going back.

why eating organic helps

Even if you are making a real effort to stick to a balanced, healthy diet, the nutrient content of many nonorganic foods is known to be less in practice than it is in theory. Produce that has been grown in poor soil, picked before it is ripe, and then kept in cold storage for long periods loses much of its nutritional value, as do highly processed, pre-packaged convenience foods.

It is my belief that you will increase your nutrient intake by switching to organic produce wherever possible. Fresh organic produce grown in good organic soil is likely to have higher vitamin and mineral content than its nonorganic counterpart, and so it will help build healthier bodies and stronger immune systems. In the same way, there is every probability that eggs, dairy products, meat, and poultry from animals reared on organic feed or pasture will be nutritionally richer. These products are also known to be free of residues from the antibiotics that are routinely fed to animals as growth promoters by conventional farmers. There is considerable concern that our consumption of animal antibiotics may lead to resistant strains of bacteria in people and consequently reduce the effectiveness of our bodies' own defense mechanisms.

To date, there simply hasn't been enough scientific research into the differences between organic foods and conventionally farmed produce to provide absolute proof that organic foods are safer and more nutritious, but I have no doubt that it is only a matter of time until there is ample evidence to support my firm belief that this is so.

There are certainly useful health benefits in eating the meat from free-range cattle. Not only does free-range beef contain less saturated fat than intensively reared livestock, but it also has higher levels of a naturally occurring fatty acid called conjugated linoleic acid (CLA). CLA aids in the efficient transportation, storage, and metabolism of fats in the body but is frequently deficient in humans, even in those who eat a healthy diet.

Professor Mike Pariza at the University of Wisconsin, Madison, discovered CLA more than 20 years ago when he was researching the potential carcinogenic properties of fried hamburgers. He isolated CLA from free-range beef and found that it was anti-carcinogenic. He has been researching the properties of this special fatty acid ever since and found that it is a key factor in weight management, as it helps reduce total body fat and increase muscle tone as part of an enzyme reaction that breaks down fat globules in the blood.

Only by eating meat and dairy products from free-range cattle can you be certain of getting an adequate input of CLA and all its benefits. All certified-organic cattle must be raised free range. An additional and vital factor to bear in mind regarding beef is that there has not been a single case in Great Britain of BSE (bovine spongiform encephalopathy) in an animal bred on an organic farm from a wholly organic mother. The practice of feeding cattle animal by-products— the probable cause of BSE—is not allowed on organic farms.

Another reason to choose organic beef and meat products is to avoid unwanted growth hormones and antibiotics in your meat. While the use of growth hormones is controversial—their use is banned in most of Europe but approved by the USDA and other countries—you can simply avoid the whole issue by going organic.

It is particularly important that couples planning pregnancy, pregnant and breastfeeding women, and babies eat organic dairy foods. This may mean financial sacrifice, but I don't believe it is one that any responsible parent can afford not to make. The sensitivity of the fetus and baby to neurotoxic chemicals, growth hormones, and antibiotics is well documented, and although scientific evidence of fetal damage or serious health consequences in babies is not widely established, the theoretical risks are far greater than many others that have become national issues.

There is no evidence that any of these agrochemicals is safe for the baby in the womb or the small child, and if most of these substances were to be put through the medical licensing requirements by the U.S. Food and Drug Administration (FDA), I doubt that they would have gotten onto the market.

The contamination of mothers' milk with agrochemical residues and antibiotics also presents a hazard to the health of babies. In 1999 the World Wide Fund for Nature published a report that identified more than 350 pollutants in breast milk. The report called for governments to reduce levels of suspect chemicals used by industry, including pesticides used on farms. One of the most dangerous of these chemicals is lindane, which has suspected links to breast cancer. Although its use is banned or severely restricted in nearly 40 countries, this compound is not banned in the United States or Great Britain. However, lindane is no longer manufactured in the United States, and its use in U.S. agriculture has been significantly curtailed. However, other countries still allow its use, and produce and dairy products imported to the United States can contain traces of this substance.

A leading fetal and infant toxicology expert has gone public on the importance of organic foods during pre-conceptual planning, pregnancy, breastfeeding, infancy, and early childhood. Dr. Vyvyan Howard of the University of Liverpool has stated, "One of the most positive things we can do is eat organic food. This considerably reduces the 'body burden' of toxic chemicals in both parent and child. Organic food in its many forms avoids all the possible exposures to pesticides during growing, harvesting, and storing food before you eat it."

Unwanted chemical residues and harmful antibiotics are health risks. Can there be any better reason for buying organic for all your fresh produce? Beyond that, it is just as important to choose organic when consuming manufactured foods because the nonorganic versions will contain artificial food colorings and flavorings, preservatives, artificial sweeteners, and any number of other additives. More than 3,000 chemicals are approved for food use by government agencies, but the safety of some of them is still open to question, and their effects on small children and on those with allergies is very worrisome. Chemicals in food are a common cause of allergies such as asthma and eczema, as well as behavioral disturbances like attention deficit disorder (ADD). As long as doubts remain about the safety of any of the chemicals used in the production of food or in the food processing industry, I prefer to adopt the precautionary principle and choose organic whenever possible.

the power of the green dollar

Although, in global terms, the total market for organic produce is comparatively small, the growth in the acreage of organic farmland and in the total sales of organic food have both been dramatic in recent years. Even the most casual observer could not fail to see that there is increasingly widespread concern throughout the United States and Europe over the presence of chemicals in the food chain.

As people worldwide have become more alarmed about the effects of chemical farming and the demand for organic food has continued to grow, the consumer-led revolution has prompted a rapid expansion of certified organic farmland to more than 18 million acres around the world. This increase in production has allowed the overall market for organic food to reach an estimated $6 billion in the United States and $22 billion worldwide in 1999. It is estimated that the U.S. market alone will be $100 billion by 2005. According to U.S. Agriculture Secretary Dan Glickman, organic farming is one of the fastest-growing segments of U.S. agriculture during the 1990s, and the number of organic farmers in the United States is growing by about 12 percent per year. It's obvious that consumers' concerns are the driving force behind this expanding business. And it is likely that this will drive up the number of farms turning to organic production even more rapidly in the coming years.

These figures all relate to certified organic land. There are many more acres going through the conversion process (which takes a minimum of 2 years), a multitude of farms that are partially organic, and thousands of acres in developing countries where there is no certification facility.

The percentage of organic farmland in the United States still lags behind—it accounts for just 0.2 percent of the total—but in a recent announcement by the USDA on its National Organic Standards, a plan was revealed to help small producers in 15 states receive organic certification. Currently, about half the nation's organic producers aren't certified, so the number of acres farmed organically should increase dramatically in the near future.

biodiversity

One of the greatest arguments against chemical agriculture and genetically modified (GM) foods is the case for the preservation of biodiversity. Despite claims to the contrary by governments and big business with vested interests, there is mounting evidence of the detrimental effects of intensive agricultural practices on wildlife.

One British study published in May 2000 summarized the biodiversity benefits of organic farming. The report highlights the worrying decline of biodiversity on British farms and compares the much wider spread of species found on organic farms as compared to conventional farms. Organic farm fields contain five times as many wild plants and 57 percent more species, 25 percent more birds around the edges of fields and 44 percent more in the fields during autumn and winter, three times as many butterflies, up to five times as many spiders, and almost twice the number of insects that provide food for the birds. Still, there were no more of the pest butterfly varieties and fewer aphids on organic farms than on conventional farms. While a similar study hasn't been done in the United States, there's little doubt that the results of such a study would be similar to the one done in Britain.

Organic cereals are a vitally important part of the whole organic equation, as the intensive monocropping of conventionally farmed grains is a major source of soil erosion and the development of the huge dust bowls that now cover many thousands of acres of once-fertile land in the United States. These "deserts," the original sites that author Rachel Carson drew attention to in her 1962 book on ecology, *Silent Spring*, can return to fertility and renewed biodiversity if they are cultivated using organic methods.

If you think it is only the chemicals that kill insects, birds, and mammals, think again. In August 2000 scientists from the Iowa State University carried out field studies that confirmed previous laboratory studies published in *Nature*, a weekly international journal of science, and showed that genetically modified BT (*Bacillus thuringiensis*, a botanical pesticide) pollen could kill monarch butterfly caterpillars. Pollen from fields of BT corn drifted onto nearby plants of milkweed—the caterpillar's favorite food—and the concentration on those plants nearest to the genetically modified crops was sufficient to kill the caterpillars. Lower levels found on more distant milk thistles did not appear to affect the caterpillars or subsequent butterflies.

Organic farmers have long maintained that growing a range of crops reduces the risks of disease. The importance of biodiversity is illustrated by another piece of research published in *Nature*. Chinese farmers in the Yunnan province were persuaded to plant a mixture of two different types of rice. The more valuable but immensely vulnerable sticky rice was planted between blocks of disease-resistant standard rice that acted as a protective barrier. The diverse planting

Organic farming methods help maintain the biodiversity of the countryside as well as support greater numbers of wildlife than conventional methods of farming.

resulted in greater yields per acre of both crops and such dramatic reductions in fungal disease that farmers were able to stop using most fungicides. With 100,000 acres under cultivation, the scale of this study makes the results extremely important. They suggest that mixed planting is a simple and effective nonchemical method of controlling a major disease in a staple food crop, and could be the way forward for other heavily sprayed crops. Two such candidates for this approach—barley crops in Europe and coffee grown in Colombia—are under investigation.

finding organic foods

The explosion in demand for organic foods seems to have taken everyone by surprise. More stores are carrying it or even specializing in it, but the supplies still haven't caught up with the growing demand. According to a report by CNN (Cable News Network), the organic food market is undersaturated, meaning the demand for products is greater than what's available to fill customers' needs. Whole Foods, America's largest natural food store chain with 47 stores, had revenues of more than $500 million back in 1995. Seeing the growing market for this type of food, it purchased its chief rival and added another $200 million of revenue to its bottom line. Organic foods are popular—so popular that many people are willing to pay up to 20 percent more for organic than other food.

Demand for organic foods is just as strong elsewhere in the world. Every major supermarket chain in England now stocks a wide range of organic fresh produce as well as a great variety of groceries such as flour, cereals, breads, canned goods, poultry, eggs, dairy products, juices, and wines. Organic baby foods now outsell conventional brands in many areas. England's major frozen food retailer, Iceland, has guaranteed that all its own brand frozen vegetables are organic and will not cost any more than the branded

nonorganics—a true sign that organic eating is no longer only for the affluent elite but has become a serious concern for ordinary people doing their everyday shopping.

Rising concerns about the unacceptable way intensively reared animals are kept, coupled with food scares linking BSE (mad cow disease), salmonella, and listeria to intensive farming methods, have made more and more people turn to organic meat and poultry. These items are commonly available in supermarkets (although they are noticeably more expensive), and there is a growing number of organic butcher shops and organic farms selling naturally reared and chemical-free chicken, turkey, goose, duck, beef, and lamb direct to the public—many via the Internet. Organically reared and naturally produced ham, bacon, and sausages are now available, too.

It takes at least two whole generations of being raised organically before livestock can actually be sold as organic. However, thanks to the increasing number of organic herds, the amount of organic milk—from cows, sheep, and goats—has risen dramatically, and this means a much wider availability of organic cheeses, yogurts, cream, and butter. Grains, pasta, and all types of beans are universally available in organic forms and are ideal sources of protein and energy for people on a tight budget.

Organic is no bar to the use of frozen foods, and it is worth remembering that good quality organic frozen vegetables may contain even higher levels of nutrients than fresh equivalents that have been badly stored. Ready-made frozen meals are not recommended on a daily basis, but there are times when they can really be a lifesaver. The good news is that organic frozen meals are now on the market although they are not yet widely available.

Organic food is now so popular that more unusual foods—such as sun-dried tomatoes and exotic mushrooms—can be found together with the organic staples.

Finding out whether food is organic isn't always easy. Standards vary from place to place, and labeling hasn't always been consistent. However, in early 2001 the U.S. Department of Agriculture (USDA) adopted strict guidelines for labeling organic foods, making it much easier for the consumer to know what it is they are really buying. Prior to that, organic labeling depended largely upon where in the world you live, with 44 different state and organic certifying organizations in the United States alone!

When buying organic foods, you should check that the product is labeled as organic. The new USDA Organic seal for foods whose ingredients are at least 95 percent organic will make it easier to make your selections; however, the program isn't slated to take full effect until 2002. Seeing this label on the food you buy ensures that, in addition to using no synthetic pesticides and fertilizers in the growing of produce and no use of antibiotics or growth hormones in organic meat, the ingredients cannot be exposed to irradiation, biotechnology, or sewer-sludge fertilizer. There are four categories of organic food, labeled as follows:

★ "100 percent organic": must contain only organic ingredients

★ "Organic": ingredients must be at least 95 percent organic

★ "Made with organic ingredients": must contain at least 70 percent organic ingredients

★ The fourth category includes packaged foods that contain less than 70 percent organic ingredients. These foods may not be labeled as organic, although the organic ingredients may be labeled as such on the information panel.

Demand for organic food is increasing at such a dramatic rate and farming in general is in such decline that there is a huge rush of both agricultural and horticultural producers into the organic market. But going organic is not simple. It takes a minimum of 2 years of transition to obtain organic accreditation. During this period no herbicides are allowed on the farm, and the use of synthetic chemicals is severely restricted. The management of livestock is changed to ensure free-range systems and nonreliance on antibiotics, de-wormers, and other veterinary treatments, and the animals' feeds are based on fully organic rations. Lastly, the producers have to learn all the new skills involved.

The transition period can be a very difficult time for farmers as their productivity falls, but they can't yet sell their products as certified organic, which means they can't earn premium prices. Some supermarkets are now selling "transitional" foods, including vegetables, meat, eggs, and dairy products. The grocery stores pay the farmers a small premium over conventionally grown products and sell the goods for less than the price of certified organic products.

Caveat emptor—let the buyer beware—is the attitude that you should adopt as a consumer. There is certainly far more "organic" and "in transition" produce on sale than it would be possible to produce on land that is certified organic or formally in transition. While there are many genuine small producers that may not have the resources for formal certification, there are others who are less scrupulous—so do make sure you ask the vendors at the farmers' market whether their goods have been produced according to organic principles, and check with your supermarket manager as to the sources of their products.

As the organic movement grows and changes from a cottage industry into a multimillion-dollar international business, the multinational corporations are jumping on the bandwagon. Consequently, a trickle of organic junk food has begun creeping into the supermarkets. My fear is that this will soon become a raging torrent. A high-fat, high-sugar, or high-salt organic product may be marginally better for you than its nonorganic equivalent, but heart disease is heart disease whether it is caused by organic or nonorganic junk food.

The higher price of organic food used to be a problem for most consumers, but the situation is improving as demand grows and supply increases to match it. Organic food is necessarily more costly to produce than conventionally farmed equivalents, but prices of many organic foods have fallen in recent years. Indeed, the market for organic dairy products has become so large that organic yogurts are now the same price as nonorganic in some supermarkets.

The outlook for organic food in the future is incredibly positive. More than 18 million acres of land are now being farmed organically worldwide, and in Europe, trends indicate that 30 percent of all farming may be organic by the year 2010. In June 2000 San Francisco city officials announced that they want organic food vendors in their city, not vendors who may be selling genetically modified foods. And it's projected that 10 million customers will buy $8 billion worth of organic food this year in the United States.

You may think that you have no access to a good supply of organic food where you live. You will almost certainly be wrong. Small specialty shops, organic sections in supermarkets, health-food stores, and farmers' markets are spreading throughout the United States. But even if one of these is not on your corner or within easy access, there are two new developments that have revolutionized organic shopping—home delivery and the Internet.

The Internet is a cornucopia of wonderful organic food suppliers, recipes, and anything you want to know about organic growing, buying, cooking, and eating—all available at the click of a mouse. The briefest search on my computer found www.orgfood.com, which is the site of Organic Provisions, a Pennsylvania company that provides a mail-order service for a vast range of organic foods (including baby food and pet food), clothing, and domestic products, as well as an extraordinary list of kosher organic foods. A few clicks more found 18 links to other organic food sites. No matter where you are in the world you will find something similar. Everything from meat, potatoes, dairy products, fruit, and vegetables to wine, cookies, cakes, and juices can be delivered right to your doorstep, regardless of where you live.

organic eating for health

In nutritional terms, going organic has never been more important. The best protection from unwanted and unseen ingredients can be yours if you use as much organic food as possible in your daily diet. Eating organic is your best guarantee of avoiding the hidden antibiotics that lead to resistant strains of bacteria; the chemical residues that may cause nerve damage; food additives that can trigger asthma, eczema, and hyperactive behavior in children; and all the other food chemicals that could be detrimental to your health and that of your family.

Don't lose heart if you can't find or can't afford to switch to a completely organic diet. Incorporate as much organic food as you can, and remember: Nonorganic fruit and vegetables are infinitely better for you than no fruit and vegetables at all.

The basis for sensible eating is a varied diet with plenty of fruit, vegetables, and whole grains. Quite simply, the wider the variety of foods that you and your family eat, the less chance there is of missing out on vital nutrients. Living on a diet of junk food and making up for it by taking vitamin pills simply won't work. Vitamin supplements contain only the nutrients scientists already know about; without doubt, there are many more substances in food that have yet to be isolated and identified. Until they are, they certainly won't crop up in vitamin pills.

Another common fallacy is the idea that a low-calorie diet has to be better for you. Low-calorie diets—even if they are organic—are a common cause of nutritional deficiency if maintained for a long time. It is difficult for a woman to consume enough food on 1,500 calories (2,000 for a man) to

(continued on page 43)

following pages: *A healthy diet should include five daily portions of fruit and vegetables, with plenty of dark green, yellow, and orange produce for beta-carotene.*

A HEALTHY DIET

★ One-third of your food should be fresh—preferably organic—fruits, salads, and vegetables (raw or cooked). Eat five portions a day (about 1½ pounds in weight) for a good daily dose of vitamins, minerals, and dietary fiber, as well as heart disease– and cancer-fighting phytonutrients.

★ One-third of your food should be potatoes, whole-grain bread and pasta, whole grains (rice, millet, and oats), beans, lentils, and other legumes for slow-release carbohydrates, fiber, B vitamins, and minerals—and protection from heart disease.

★ If you're a meat eater, get most of your protein from fish, seafood, poultry, or game; limit red meat and eggs.

★ Dairy products are the major source of calcium in most diets, but use them with common sense. Choose low-fat products, and eat no more than two or three portions a day. Small amounts of pure, natural butter are better than margarine, which has the same amount of calories but also harmful trans fats.

★ Avoid expensive processed foods and use homemade soups, vegetable casseroles, and beans as alternatives to meat. Limit all meat, especially processed meat products such as sausage, hot dogs, burgers, and lunch meats, which contain huge amounts of hidden fats.

★ Boost your immune system with some pumpkin seeds or a serving of shellfish every day for zinc, and three Brazil nuts for selenium.

★ Beta-carotene and vitamins C and E are essential antioxidants that defend every cell in the body from attack, so eat plenty of fruit, salads, and dark green, yellow, and orange produce, as well as avocados, cold-pressed olive oil, and nut oils.

provide the full spectrum of vitamins, minerals, trace elements, and phytonutrients necessary for healthy living. Follow some simple guidelines (see "A Healthy Diet" on page 40) and you will achieve optimum nutrition with minimum effort and a reasonable caloric intake.

In our modern society, we go all out for convenience, so daily shopping is usually out of the question. Be sure to buy vegetables that will stay fresh for a few days, such as potatoes, carrots, and onions, and store them in brown paper bags in a cool, dark place. Keep supplies of salad ingredients such as peppers, celery, fennel, and watercress in the refrigerator, and grow alfalfa or bean sprouts in a dark corner of your kitchen. Sprouts provide a useful helping of protein, B vitamins, and minerals that is organically grown, fresh, additive free—and cheap, too.

When you cannot find organic fruit and vegetables, the next best thing is to buy nonorganic produce and wash it thoroughly with a product like Fit (a fruit and vegetable wash made of natural, plant-based ingredients) or a weak solution of dishwashing liquid (1 teaspoon per 3 cups of warm water), and then rinse under running water. This will remove a large proportion of the surface residues and waxes. Fruit and vegetables are so important to your health that it is always better to eat them in some form each day, even if they have to be nonorganic.

The basic rules of good nutrition apply throughout life, but the body's needs for particular nutrients change as we grow and age. Turn to the section appropriate to your age or your family members' ages in the following pages to find out more about the foods that are good for each of you.

infancy

For the first 4 to 6 months of life, breast milk is best: It boosts natural immunity and reduces the risk of infection. If a mother is eating organically, her milk will be organic and free from harmful residues. Of course, not all women are able to breastfeed, and those who have difficulties should simply use organic formulas to avoid giving their babies a cocktail of unwanted chemicals.

Eating three Brazil nuts a day supplies the body's daily requirement of selenium, an antioxidant that helps provide protection from heart disease and stroke.

FOOD ADDITIVES AND HIVES

If your child suffers from frequent attacks of hives or rashes, switching to organic food could solve the problem as quickly as switching off a light. There is a specific group of food additives that are probably the most common cause of hives in children. Below are some of the most common additives in the commercial food industry, which are heavily used in many products aimed specifically at the children's market. None of these are allowed in the manufacture of organic foods.

Tartrazine
Sunset yellow
Amaranth
Ponceau 4R
Sorbic acid
Sodium sorbate
Potassium sorbate
Calcium sorbate
Benzoic acid
Sodium benzoate
Potassium benzoate
Calcium benzoate
Ethyl 4-hydroxybenzoate
Sodium ethyl 4-hydroxybenzoate
Propyl 4-hydroxybenzoate
Sodium propyl 4-hydroxybenzoate

In my experience, avoiding the chemical colorings and preservatives on this list may alleviate your child's allergic reactions.

Once infants graduate to other foods, the easiest way to feed them organically is by giving them the same foods you cook for yourself. If lifestyle constrictions make this impossible, however, don't fret: Excellent organically produced baby foods are now available.

Introduce babies to some organic, puréed, unsalted vegetables and unsugared fruits when they are between 4 and 5 months old. At around 6 months, start feeding them organic rice, mashed potatoes, or plain yogurt—but take care with cow's milk, wheat-based products, eggs, nuts, nut butters, and citrus fruits, as these are the most common causes of allergic reactions in babies.

Offering babies a wide range of food tastes and textures helps them to develop much more tolerant palates, as well as providing them with the widest possible range of vitamins and minerals. In fact, a child who eats brussels sprouts by the age of 7 months will probably eat anything in later life.

All food for babies should be organic if at all possible. As well as being free from all the chemicals used in agriculture, organic food is also free from other artificial additives such as sweeteners. One study shows that many children less than 5 years old swallow more saccharin a day than the recommended safe intake for adults.

childhood and adolescence

These are years of growth, development, and hormonal change, demanding the best possible nutrition. Growing children are particularly vulnerable to chemical residues in food because their nervous and immune systems are immature and more susceptible to damage. Organic foods—particularly dairy products—have an important role to play in protecting children from exposure to unwanted chemicals that can cause allergic reactions and behavioral disorders.

Youngsters need all the energy they can get to help them enjoy the fun—and cope with the stresses—of busy, exciting, and active lives. Give them foods rich in vitamin B, such as whole-grain cereals (including oatmeal and muesli), liver, meat, chicken, fish, and leafy vegetables. Add whole grains and pumpkin seeds for zinc, which maintains healthy growth and skin; liver and dark green leafy vegetables for iron, which builds healthy blood and aids mental performance; and dairy products for calcium, to develop strong bones.

With the onset of menstruation, teenage girls are especially in need of iron. Vitamin C aids the absorption of

Encourage your children to eat clementines and other citrus fruits: They are excellent sources of vitamin C, which aids the absorption of iron and helps heal wounds.

FOODS FOR CHILDHOOD AND ADOLESCENCE

Dates: High in potassium and a good source of slow-release carbohydrate for energy

Eggs: Useful source of protein (supplying around $1/8$ ounce per egg) and of iron, zinc, B vitamins, and vitamin D

Lentils: Good source of protein, with more than 1 ounce per $3\frac{1}{2}$-ounce serving. Eating food rich in vitamin C at the same meal will aid in the iron absorption from lentils.

Oatmeal: Supplies iron, zinc, calcium, and B vitamins, and is a good source of slow-release carbohydrate for energy

Oranges: The vitamin C in a whole, fresh orange eaten at the start of a meal boosts the absorption of iron.

Parsley: Excellent source of beta-carotene, vitamin C, and iron if eaten in sufficient quantity

Pumpkin seeds: Valuable source of B vitamins as well as iron, zinc, and unsaturated fatty acids

Spinach: High in beta-carotene, which is essential for night vision and is also a powerful antioxidant that protects against heart disease and some forms of cancer; useful source of potassium and folic acid

iron, so encourage them to drink fresh fruit juice instead of carbonated beverages and to eat plenty of citrus fruits or fruit salads.

Excess weight often worries teenagers but no one—regardless of age—should diet without professional advice. It is especially important that teenagers steer clear of all fad diets, as they can seriously damage their health at this age. An obsession with weight can also lead to more serious problems such as anorexia and bulimia.

the twenties

At this age the days are never long enough. You need food that protects against stress of every kind: work, romance, partying, and too much snacking on junk food. Eating healthily can also

The silicon in cauliflower and other brassicas such as broccoli and cabbage will keep your skin firm and your hair strong.

FOODS FOR THE TWENTIES

Avocados: Easily digestible, filling, and rich in vitamin E

Bananas: Contain vitamin B_6 and potassium to help alleviate the symptoms of premenstrual syndrome (PMS)

Carrots: Just one supplies the entire daily requirement of beta-carotene.

Cauliflower: Supplies silicon for strong bones, healthy hair, and firm skin

Potatoes: Good news for weight watchers—one large baked potato, with its crispy skin, contains only about 150 calories and is a valuable source of vitamin C, slow-release carbohydrate, fiber, folic acid, and minerals

Salmon: Contains omega-3 essential oils—the good fats that have a strongly protective action on the heart

Sunflower seeds: Packed with B vitamins, vitamin E, minerals, unsaturated fats, and protein

Thyme: Its antibacterial properties are great for acne.

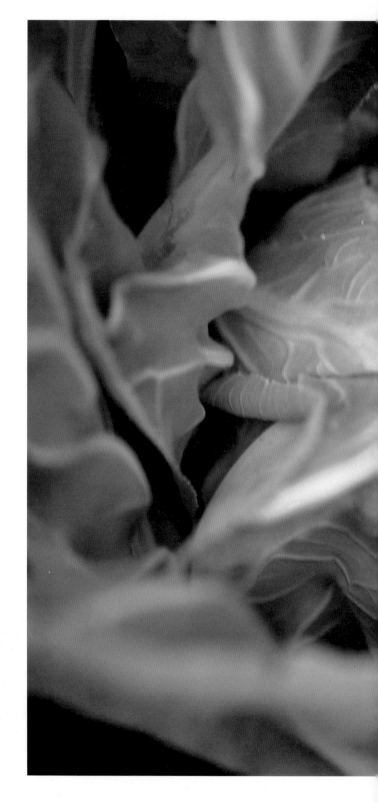

EAT HEALTHY AT WORK

The condition known as sick office syndrome (SOS) is the result of a combination of factors: ozone emissions from office equipment, pollution from paints and other synthetic preparations, low levels of humidity, and infection spread by air conditioning.

To combat SOS, eat foods high in carotenoids—nutrients that protect the delicate lining of the nose, sinuses, throat, and lungs. The best known of the carotenoids is beta-carotene, the ingredient that gives carrots their color, but there are many others essential for optimum protection.

If you work in an office environment, be sure to eat a generous portion of at least two of the following every day.

Apricots (fresh or dried)

Blackberries

Blueberries

Broccoli

Cantaloupe

Carrots

Lettuce (dark green or red)

Peppers (yellow or red)

Prunes

Spinach

Sweet potatoes

Spring greens

Strawberries

Tomatoes

Watercress

help women overcome menstrual problems. Eat plenty of whole-grain cereals, nuts, and seeds for magnesium, B vitamins, vitamin E, and iron. Skin problems such as acne are devastating in your twenties. Choose one day a week to eat nothing but fruit and vegetables, and drink plenty of water and herbal teas; this will cleanse your system and supply many healthy essential nutrients. Avocados contain vitamin E and essential fatty acids, while cauliflower, broccoli, cabbage, spinach, watercress, and orange and red fruits and vegetables provide minerals including silicon, beta-carotene, and vitamin C.

the thirties and forties

During your thirties and forties you're in the prime of your life. You'll never have more natural energy—and you'll never need it more. You can't afford the time to be ill, so make sure you eat a healthy diet to boost your resistance to infection and disease.

To help maintain your immune system, you need a daily helping of the essential foods that provide a good supply of beta-carotene and vitamin C, B vitamins, and zinc. Eat apricots, black currants, citrus fruits, broccoli, and peppers for beta-carotene and vitamin C; sprouts and yogurt for

B vitamins; and oats, wheat germ, almonds, chicken livers, eggs, poultry, game, and oily fish like salmon, sardines, mackerel, and herring for B vitamins and zinc. These foods should form your basic diet. Prolonged stress is a great destroyer of defense mechanisms. Try to reduce its effects by eating carbohydrate-rich foods, which are calming. Drink lime flower tea with some honey in it to help you relax.

For the future health of your heart, eat high-fiber foods, oily fish, and vegetable proteins such as millet, buckwheat, and beans. Opt for foods rich in beta-carotene and vitamin C, such as cantaloupe and dark green leafy vegetables. Eat plenty of onions and garlic. Use cold-pressed olive oil on salads. Cut down animal fats, salt, and refined carbohydrates. If you drink alcohol, do so in moderation: no more than two glasses of wine, spirits, or beer per day. And be sure to get some form of regular weight-bearing exercise to keep your muscles toned.

For women, it is not uncommon for PMS symptoms to become worse after they have children. To help counteract its effects, fight cravings for sugar and chocolate, and

Cheese contains calcium, essential for strong bones, but choose low-fat varieties and save Brie and Camembert for an occasional treat.

FOODS FOR THE THIRTIES AND FORTIES

Almonds: Good source of protein, unsaturated fats, zinc, magnesium, potassium, iron, and some B vitamins

Cantaloupe: A rich source of beta-carotene

Celery: Its diuretic properties are well known; eat it to reduce fluid retention associated with your period.

Cheese: Good source of protein, calcium, and phosphorus, as well as vitamin A, B vitamins, and some vitamin D and E. Feta, cottage, and curd cheese are low in fat.

Grapes: Easy to digest and high in natural sugars and vitamin C, grapes provide powerful antioxidant flavonoids—the unique plant chemicals that help protect the body against many diseases.

Sage: A powerful healing and antiseptic herb

Sardines: Rich in protein, vitamins D and B_{12}, calcium, iron, and zinc—every woman's friend

Sprouts: Grow this source of protein, B vitamins, and minerals right on your windowsill.

instead choose sweet fruits such as grapes and melon or dried fruit and almonds. Increase your intake of vitamin B$_6$ from oily fish, whole-grain cereals, and bananas. You will need more zinc and magnesium from pumpkin seeds, chickpeas, kidney beans, liver, shellfish, and mackerel. Cut down on caffeine and alcohol—or cut them out entirely.

Strong bones need calcium and vitamin D (found mainly in sunlight), which is essential to its absorption. Eat at least three of the following each day for calcium: cabbage, celery, spinach, turnips, dried fruits, seeds, nuts, brown rice, buckwheat, chickpeas, herring, sardines (including the bones), tuna, eggs, low-fat cheese, yogurt, and skim milk. Fish, eggs, and milk also contain vitamin D.

the fifties

The different physiologies of men and women mean that they have different needs in terms of nutrition throughout their lives. While the balanced diets described earlier are good for both sexes, during the latter years of life it is important to focus on the particular needs of each sex in order to enjoy a healthy older age. Good nutrition for men is even more crucial as they get older since a man is more than twice as likely to have a heart attack or a stroke between the ages of 55 and 74 than a woman of the same age. Once women reach menopause, they are also at greater risk of suffering a stroke or heart attack than in their earlier years.

eating for a healthy heart

A balanced diet that preferably includes plenty of organic produce can reduce the risk of heart disease, high blood pressure, and stroke in both men and women. Increasing the amount of fiber—particularly soluble fiber that comes from oats, beans, apples, bananas, citrus fruits, pears, and root vegetables—is a great starting point. Vitamin C is important, as it reduces the risk of blood clots, so eat plenty of red, green, and yellow peppers, kiwis, oranges, and black currants. Garlic is good for reducing cholesterol (eat 1 to 3 raw cloves daily), as is lecithin from soybeans and liver. Fresh fruit, carrots, and dark green leafy vegetables

Apples are a good source of soluble fiber, which lowers blood cholesterol levels and stabilizes blood sugar levels.

will help protect your body against heart disease and keep your veins and arteries in good condition.

Throw away the salt shaker—the silent killer on your kitchen table—and cut down on all foods that contain salt to help reduce high blood pressure. The American Heart Association advises that you limit salt intake to less than 6 grams per day. Much of our salt consumption comes from hidden sources such as processed and ready-made foods, so read the labels before you buy packaged foods. Many cardiologists now recommend limiting the amount of added table salt to 4 grams daily to allow for this extra intake.

Modest exercise, such as a 20-minute walk 3 times a week, a sensible alcohol consumption (no more than two glasses of red wine a day), together with a regular intake of raw garlic, good olive oil, and oily fish will all help to keep you young at heart.

nutrition for men: eating for a longer life

At any age, men have a greater requirement for some nutrients than women. As a rule, they need more calories, protein, magnesium, zinc, selenium, thiamin (B_1), riboflavin (B_2), niacin (B_3), pyridoxine (B_6), and vitamin A. Because the risk for nutrition-based diseases such as heart disease, osteoporosis, and diabetes increases as you grow older, be sure to choose plenty of foods listed in "Foods for Men in Their Fifties" on this page.

nutrition for women: easing menopause symptoms

There is no need to dread the onset of menopause. Although symptoms of menopause can be unpleasant and distressing, simply changing your eating habits may be enough to control them (see "Foods for Menopause" on page 55).

Hot flashes, like other symptoms such as headaches, skin problems, and sexual difficulties, are caused by a reduction in the levels of the hormone estrogen. Vitamin E helps relieve these symptoms. Good sources of vitamin E are vegetable oils, nuts and

(continued on page 56)

right: *Garlic is particularly beneficial in later life; it helps reduce the levels of cholesterol in the blood and provides protection against heart disease.*
following pages: *Pumpkin seeds and dried fruits are packed with nutrients that may help relieve menopausal symptoms.*

FOODS FOR MEN IN THEIR FIFTIES

Artichokes: Eating at least two artichokes a week does wonders for the liver and gall bladder. One of the natural ingredients in artichokes is cynarin, which stimulates bile production and liver function—a benefit for men with a long history of alcohol consumption or a tendency to gallstones.

Brazil nuts: Three shelled Brazil nuts a day provide the 70 micrograms of selenium essential for heart health and protection against prostate cancer.

Garlic: Essential for protection against heart disease, cholesterol, high blood pressure, and blood clots, garlic has the bonus of being antibacterial and antifungal. Eat at least one raw clove a day; three cloves is even better.

Red meat: Useful in small quantities for its iron and B vitamins, particularly vitamin B_{12}. Muscle strength declines with age in men, and the easily absorbed protein and iron in lean red meat help maintain healthy blood and strong muscle tissue.

Salmon: The only organically farmed oily fish other than trout, salmon is expensive, but the essential fatty acids protect against heart disease.

Shellfish: Shellfish are a good source of zinc.

Watercress: Vital for smokers or ex-smokers because it contains phenethyl isothiocyanate, which appears to inhibit the proliferation of lung cancer cells. Also a good source of iron, vitamin C, and chlorophyll to boost the immune system. Choose organic to avoid the chemical pollution in the water in commercial watercress beds.

Yogurt: Improves digestion and boosts the immune system; yogurt with live cultures is most beneficial.

FOODS FOR MENOPAUSE

Chickpeas: Super food that supplies protein and some B vitamins and is a useful source of iron and potassium as well as calcium, zinc, magnesium, and phosphorus

Nuts: Almonds and hazelnuts are a good source of vitamin E, calcium, magnesium, iron, and zinc.

Oats: Good source of easily digested protein, soluble fiber, B vitamins, vitamin E, magnesium, potassium, and silicon

Peppers: Excellent source of vitamin C; the red and yellow ones also provide a good supply of beta-carotene.

Red beets: Beets contain iron and are a good source of folic acid, which makes them a valuable addition to a menopause diet. Use both the root and the leaf; they are excellent raw in salads, dressed with sunflower seed oil, lemon juice, and sprinkled with sesame seeds.

Sesame and pumpkin seeds: Good source of protein, iron, zinc, calcium, magnesium, and potassium; sunflower seeds and pine kernels are also excellent sources of vitamin E.

Soy beans: Rich in fiber, protein, and the vitally important phyto-estrogens

Spring greens: A real lifesaver during menopause, greens contain potassium, calcium, and iron, and are a rich source of beta-carotene, vitamin C, and folic acid.

Vegetable oils: Wheat germ oil and other types of oils are good sources of vitamin E and unsaturated fatty acids.

nut oils, and seeds. Soybeans are rich in plant estrogens, which help ease most menopausal difficulties. Going organic is even more important when it comes to soy to avoid genetically modified beans.

Next to hot flashes, depression is the most common menopausal problem. Calcium, magnesium, and the amino acid tryptophan may help reduce symptoms. You can get them all from organic dairy products, spinach, sesame seeds, almonds, cashews, whole-grain flour, brown rice, chickpeas, soybeans, bananas, dried fruits, and seafood. B vitamins are vital from liver, oily fish, whole-grain cereals, eggs, spinach, and yeast extracts. Eat two foods from this group each day.

Aching joints are often a problem in later years. Eating plenty of turnips helps eliminate the uric acid that can cause these aches and pains.

You can help yourself to better bones even after menopause has begun by taking in more calcium, magnesium, zinc, and vitamin D. Eat nuts and seeds for their mineral content, as well as sardines, yogurt, and low-fat cheese for vitamin D. Vary your choices or choose just your favorites but eat some of these foods each day, and be sure to do some form of weight-bearing exercise regularly.

the sixties and beyond

Today, we can reasonably expect to live until the age of 75. Although the brain loses cells as it grows older, the muscles lose some strength, the joints some flexibility, the digestion some tolerance, and the eyes and ears some sharpness, these are the normal processes and consequences of living. With a positive attitude toward life—and plenty of attention to

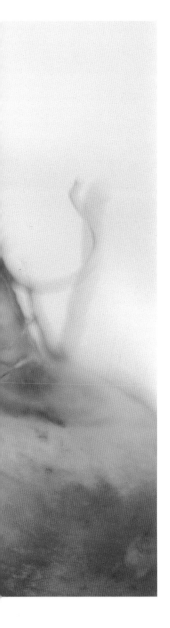

FOODS FOR THE SIXTIES AND BEYOND

Chicken: A great form of protein that is low in fat when eaten without the skin, chicken is easier to find in organic form than other meats, is quick and easy to cook, and offers good nutritional value for money. Buy free-range birds if you can. Make soup from the leftovers, adding lots of green and root vegetables for a highly nutritious broth.

Chicory: This herb stimulates the gall bladder to produce bile, which makes it an aid to liver function and digestion.

Dried fruits: A superb source of energy, apricots are high in soluble fiber, beta-carotene, potassium, magnesium, iron, and folic acid. Figs are a good source of soluble fiber, iron, and calcium.

Garlic: The great-granddaddy of all therapeutic food plants. Put it into savory dishes, and if you get a cold, eat it raw or roasted on toast.

Millet: Easy to digest, millet contains silicon, which is needed for the skin, hair, nails, and for the health of the walls of blood vessels.

Parsley: This herb is mildly diuretic, so it helps joints to eliminate uric acid. Drink a couple of glasses of parsley tea each day: Chop 2 teaspoons of fresh parsley, add boiling water, cover and let steep for 5 minutes, then strain and drink.

Pears: Contain some vitamin C in the skin as well as fruit sugar for rapid energy. They also contain potassium, which is important if you are taking diuretic pills (water tablets), are very easy to digest, and are a source of pectin, a soluble fiber.

Strawberries: Due to their cleansing and purifying action, strawberries are a great help for all the joint diseases.

Turnips: Powerful eliminators of uric acid, turnips help relieve gout and other joint problems. They're also said to be useful for the treatment of chest infections.

what you eat—your age will not stop you from doing anything you desire. This is the time for maximum nutrition, with the emphasis on foods that supply the most nutrients in the most digestible form. Essential are high intakes of the B vitamins (especially B_{12} and folic acid); antioxidants; beta-carotene and vitamins C and E; vitamin D to help calcium absorption; and calcium, magnesium, iron, and zinc.

The B vitamins are necessary for releasing the energy from the food you eat and for the proper functioning of the entire nervous system, and that includes the brain. Liver, chicken, and sardines are good sources of B vitamins. A steady blood sugar level is also important. To achieve this, you must eat meals at regular intervals, with enough carbohydrate-rich foods to supply starches and natural sugars. Eating dried fruits such as dates, figs, and apricots every day is one way to keep your blood sugar level in check.

To keep rheumatism and arthritis at bay, add turnips, along with their leafy tops, to your diet. They help eliminate uric acid (which aggravates joint problems) as do celery and parsley. Strawberries are also good for the joints. To keep up muscle strength, you need protein; chicken is an easily digestible source. Eat oily fish such as sardines, mackerel, salmon, and trout regularly for their protein and essential fatty acids. Lentils are another good source of protein.

Chicory or globe artichokes will stimulate your liver. Whole-grain breads and cereals, dried fruits, millet, greens, and plenty of fresh fruit help with constipation. Raw garlic is a natural antibiotic and helps keep the bowels regular.

Getting your protein from fish, poultry, and low-fat dairy products will help look after your heart. Restrict your intake of fatty foods, and eat meat such as beef, pork, and lamb infrequently. Eat foods with plenty of soluble fiber,

left: *The purple eggplant is native to Southeast Asia but it's an essential ingredient of Middle Eastern and Mediterranean cooking.*
following pages: *A slice of organic whole-grain bread and honey for breakfast will help get your day off to a good start.*

such as oats, root vegetables, citrus fruits, bananas, apples, and baked beans—the fiber helps reduce the cholesterol in your blood. Garlic and olive oil have the same effect. All these foods, together with a reduction in your intake of caffeine and salt, will also help reduce blood pressure.

Exercise is as important as ever when you're older. A brisk walk every day is ideal, but do whatever you can, even if it is only some form of regular physical exertion in your bed or armchair.

the modern disease: stress

These days stress affects everyone, regardless of age or walk of life. And stress and nutrition are inseparably linked. Overproduction of stomach acid caused by stress can lead to heartburn, which makes swallowing painful and has an adverse effect on eating. Excessive stress can also shorten the time it takes for food to pass through the colon, where many nutrients are absorbed and B vitamins are synthesized. The end result of stress is a general lowering of nutritional status and a reduction in B vitamins—some of the specific nutrients responsible for the general well-being of the nervous system.

So stress is a self-perpetuating, downward spiral of poor diet, excessive stress, nutrient deficiency, worse nutrition, worse stress. The good news is that you can eat to beat stress. Naturally, you should also make use of other stress busters. Yoga, meditation, relaxation techniques, exercise, changes in lifestyle, self-discipline, and just learning to say no can all play a major part in managing stress in a holistic way. But improving your diet is the first step on the road to recovery.

When you are under stress, you need lots of foods that are calming, soothing, and mood-enhancing, and a minimum intake of those that are overstimulating. On top of the list of villains is caffeine. If you are very sensitive to this stimulant, then avoid it altogether. Eliminate cola drinks, too—even the caffeine-free ones contain so much other junk that you are

(continued on page 63)

better off without them. And watch out for some of the sports drinks and so-called "energy" drinks, many of which also contain caffeine. If small amounts of caffeine don't upset you, then have no more than one or two caffeinated beverages a day.

High-protein diets mean high mental energy diets, so they aren't a good idea for the overstressed. Instead, eat lots of the serotonin-producing foods: bananas, pineapples, walnuts, figs, tomatoes, avocados, dates, pawpaws, passionfruit, and eggplant. The staple of your diet should be complex carbohydrates such as organic whole-grain bread, pasta, rice, beans, and potatoes. Get your protein from modest amounts of fish, low-fat cheese, eggs, poultry, and perhaps a little meat. This high-carbohydrate diet is rich in tryptophan, which the body converts to serotonin, the mood-enhancing, tranquilizing hormone.

Breakfast is a key factor in a stress-busting regime and should consist of predominantly good carbohydrates such as oatmeal, unsweetened muesli, and natural whole-grain breakfast cereals. Sweeten your oatmeal with honey and dried fruits, serve breakfast cereals with pure fruit juices, and prepare your muesli in the traditional Swiss fashion by soaking it overnight in fruit juice and serving it with honey topped with fresh fruit. Finish off the meal with whole-wheat toast and honey or good-quality preserves made without additives, and you'll be set to face the day.

It's essential to be a grazer if you are under stress, so don't go more than 2 hours without a carbohydrate snack in order to keep your blood sugar on an even keel. Avoid all alcohol, but do make use of the natural destressing herbs in your cooking: basil, rosemary, lemon balm, thyme, marjoram, and lemon verbena. Use these herbs to make teas to replace ordinary black tea and coffee, both of which contain caffeine.

Herbal teas are an ideal alternative to tea, coffee, and cola drinks as they contain no caffeine—your enemy in times of stress—and often have calming properties.

Finally, the good news. You may indulge in small quantities of high-quality chocolate—the darker the better. Although it does contain some caffeine, chocolate also contains theobromine, a chemical that stimulates the release of endorphins, our feel-good hormones.

Insomnia is a common bedfellow of stress and anxiety. If you can't sleep, don't lie there trying; instead, get up and do something boring such as ironing. Get into a regular routine of always getting up at the same time, no matter how much or little sleep you've had. Don't go to bed hungry, but don't eat a large meal late at night. It's also a good idea to avoid stimulating, high-protein meals in the evening. That's the time for rice or pasta rather than a juicy steak.

A lettuce sandwich is the perfect bedtime snack, as it includes carbohydrates to stimulate the release of brain-calming hormones and lettuce, which contains mildly sedative substances that induce sleep. Avoid caffeine—both in cola drinks as well as tea and coffee (even if it is organic). If you have a juicer, you could substitute a glass of lettuce juice for the sandwich.

who needs supplements?

People who may need to take vitamin or mineral supplements include growing children and women planning pregnancy or who are pregnant, breastfeeding, or recovering from pregnancy, as well as people with chronic debilitating illness; people with mouth, throat, or digestive problems that interfere with their eating; anyone with eating disorders; patients recovering from serious illness or surgery; and, of course, the elderly, who may not be eating well.

If you're following a special diet, either for medical or ethical reasons, you may need to take dietary supplements. People with allergies who are avoiding entire food groups, such as dairy products or wheat, definitely need to supplement their diets with a good multivitamin. For dairy avoiders, supplements must include calcium and vitamin D;

for anyone with wheat allergies, all the B vitamins should be on top of the agenda; and it is essential that vegetarians and vegans supplement their diets with vitamin B_{12}.

It's always better to increase consumption of the relevant foods than to take a pill, but for those not able to eat such a varied diet, a multivitamin and mineral supplement does make a helpful alternative. But where do you start?

As a safe general rule, you should not take more than four times the Recommended Daily Allowance (RDA) of any nutrient unless it is specifically prescribed by your health-care practitioner. If you are taking a selection of vitamins, study all the labels and add up the total amount of each nutrient that you are getting. Use single supplements only with professional guidance; otherwise, it's easy to end up taking dangerously high amounts, especially of vitamins A and D.

The one exception is vitamin C; most experts agree that a daily supplement of 500 mg is vital for good health protection. Of course, the best sources of vitamin C are still the organic basics: whole grains, fresh fruits and vegetables, raw salads, and fresh herbs sprouting on the windowsill.

the future

According to a survey by the magazine *Health Which?*, more than one in four people now eat some organic food, and the people buying it rated it as healthier, safer, and tastier than equivalent products coming from conventional farms. According to the survey, 29 percent of people choose to eat some organic food, the most popular being fruit and vegetables. One in 10 occasionally bought bread, dairy products, and meat from organic sources. The overriding reason—according to 60 percent of purchasers—was health.

Half the consumers said they bought organic because it didn't contain pesticides, while slightly under half believed that it was richer in vitamins and minerals. About 9 percent were concerned about genetically modified food, and 6 percent worried about BSE and CJD, the human form of mad cow disease. Perhaps most importantly of all, 29 percent of organic buyers chose it because it tasted better. And that means they are more likely to continue buying and eating it.

The organic movement is in its infancy. Every additional person who buys a loaf of organic bread, organic free-range eggs, a bag of organic apples or potatoes, or a container of organic yogurt contributes to the growth of the whole organic market. The same is true for organic and eco-friendly household goods and building materials. Added together, these small steps increase product turnover, which means more cash flow, which means expansion and more jobs, and that all means cheaper organic products—and more of them.

As consumers demand more organic vegetables, the supermarkets must contract their suppliers to produce more, which then allows the farmers to invest in more organic acreage, to buy more organic seed, to produce more organic fertilizer, and so increase the volume of organic food produced and the area of land under organic cultivation.

The organic world is still a minnow in a world of sharks, but it is growing, thanks to the demands of more informed customers and the commitment of organic producers. This creates a truly symbiotic relationship where each feeds off the other to the benefit of both and the detriment of neither. The more you use, the better the environment you live in, and the greater the chance of survival of the farmers, horticulturists, and producers of all organic goods.

One team of scientists has worked out that although organic farms may have lower yields than conventional farms, they can still be profitable in developing countries. Can organic food feed the world? We can only wait and see.

Markets are an ideal place to buy fresh produce, and many of them now sell foods from local organic farms, including meat and dairy products as well as a wide range of fruit and vegetables.

... from the inside out

Everyone wants to look their best. But while many of us spend a considerable amount of time and money buying and applying beauty products, the most important ingredient for good skin and hair is good food. No amount of natural beauty treatment can make up for a poor diet and an unhealthy lifestyle. A balanced diet including plenty of organic food is the first step toward good health, and good health naturally leads to a more attractive appearance. Put simply, beauty starts from within.

Regular exercise is also vital for both health and beauty. As well as giving you great skin and a fit body, physical exercise releases endorphins, which act as a natural anti-depressant and stress reliever. It is well known that stress is a key factor in the relationship between health and beauty. Anxiety causes wrinkles, poor skin, and a rundown appearance, and can sometimes lead to more serious illnesses. An organic health and beauty program means taking care of your entire body—not just its various parts.

Looking good starts from within. A balanced diet of organic food helps to give you glowing skin, shining eyes, and healthy hair.

But you do need to be careful what you put on your skin. The bloom of even the healthiest skin can fade when exposed to the harsh chemicals in some cleansing and moisturizing products. Huge amounts of chemicals are used in synthetic beauty products, and their manufacture increases environmental pollution. Many of them are tested on animals, causing unnecessary suffering. But there are plenty of organic solutions to problems such as dry skin or dandruff.

If you are going organic, you are making a commitment to living holistically. And that means being aware that if you eat junk food, put synthetic cosmetics on your face, or take strong medicines to fight the symptoms of a common cold, you will upset the finely tuned balance of your body. The good news is that it has never been easier to find cruelty-free natural beauty products that are kind to both you and the environment—and there has never been a wider choice of relaxation and accompanying health techniques to ensure that you feel good and look great!

healthy beauty

Nature's pharmacy has taken the beauty world by storm in recent years—extracts from aloe vera, calendula, wild yam, marsh mallow, and evening primrose oil are just a few examples. The most up-to-date research has shown the health benefits of natural grape extracts, carotenoids, and bioflavonoids, all made from plant sources.

One of the advantages of using beauty products made from herbs, fruits, and vegetables is that they contain healing and protective phytochemicals. These are vitamins, amino acids, and naturally occurring therapeutic compounds that can all contribute to the maintenance of your skin by slowing down the aging process and protecting

it from the damaging effects of air pollution. Combined with sunscreens, these natural products can also help counteract excessive exposure to harmful ultraviolet rays from the sun.

Humans have always experimented with their physical appearance in order to improve it, but the use of chemically based cosmetics and beauty products soared during the 20th century. Not until the late 1960s and 1970s, when the natural look became more fashionable and there was an increasing interest in environmental and ecological issues, did some people begin to question the wisdom of constantly applying synthetic chemicals to their skin.

the cost to animals

The organic approach to life is not just about our own welfare; organic living means showing concern for the rest of the earth's inhabitants, too. Many people are turning to natural products rather than condoning the testing of new synthetic beauty products on animals. The enormity of the suffering inflicted by cosmetic testing on animals is horrifying. The U.S. Department of Agriculture (USDA) reported that nearly 13 million animals died in the United States between 1990 and 1997 as a result of animal testing. Many of these cosmetics tests are unnecessary since most ingredients being used have been tested before. In addition, there are plenty of known safe substances available from which to concoct new products.

The United States could do well to follow Europe's lead in reducing animal testing. In 1997, the British government declared that it would issue no new licenses to test cosmetics on animals, a stance that jolted other European Union countries into action: The European Commission announced in the spring of 2000 that it would also ban Europe's cosmetics firms from testing their products on animals. Among the companies that will be affected are L'Oréal, Procter and

Extracts of Aloe vera, *commonly known as the medicine plant, are often used in natural beauty products.*

Gamble, and Laboratoire Garnier, although some activists are concerned that products that have been tested outside Europe will still be on sale. The battle over free-trade rights and labeling issues promises to be long and hard-fought.

the cost to you

Reading a label will tell you whether a product is guaranteed not to have been tested on animals, but it will not necessarily leave you any wiser about what's inside. All beauty products, whether they're manufactured in the United States or Europe, must list their ingredients by their Latin names, if applicable. Although this sounds great in theory, the fact is that the Latin names of synthetic and natural ingredients look very similar. Even consumers who study labels regularly may not know what they mean and, consequently, have no idea what health risks they might pose.

In an industry that changes and grows as fast as the beauty industry, it is just not possible to keep track of every product coming on to the market—a fact that should and does make consumers wary. Huge numbers of chemicals go into these products and some may trigger side effects, such as allergic reactions and asthma.

Nicotine patches are sold on the premise that their chemicals are absorbed through our skin; the same premise applies to moisturizers. It is unnerving to think that we are soaking up these concoctions every day without having any idea of what is in them or what they could be doing to us.

In the United States, cosmetic manufacturers can use almost any ingredient they like since cosmetics are classified as neither food nor drugs and thus do not come under the direct control of the Food and Drug Administration (FDA). The FDA is empowered to act only if the ingredient is proven to cause harm to users. Obviously, it would be against the interests of the cosmetics industry to harm its consumers, so there is a healthy degree of self-regulation among manufacturers.

Unfortunately, even with the best self-regulation, problems are bound to arise when dealing with unnatural substances. During the 1970s, for example, a chemical called methyl methacrylate (MMA) was widely used in the manufacture and application of artificial acrylic nails until it was discovered that it caused reactions ranging from skin allergy to complete loss of the nail plate. Concern became so great that the FDA issued its first ban of a cosmetic ingredient.

The issue of synthetic perfumes is fast becoming a political hot potato, and a strong lobbying group is growing around the issue of fragrance sensitivity. The group's concern is that all fragranced products contain a cocktail of synthetic chemicals which, they believe, can potentially overload the human immune system, resulting in a wide range of problems including double vision, sinusitis, and ear pain. It seems that the reaction can be triggered by products such as scented candles and fabric conditioner, as well as by perfume (see "Eco-friendly Household Products" on page 128).

Mary Lamielle of the National Center for Environmental Health Strategies (NCEHS), a nonprofit organization dedicated to finding solutions for environmental health problems, points out that although the level of individual chemicals in perfumes and other products may be low, people rarely experience only one exposure. "These same chemicals are cropping up in many different products," she says. Obviously, perfume belongs to the ranks of scented suspects, and some employers have taken the problem sufficiently seriously to introduce "fragrance-free" zones in their offices, asking employees not to wear perfume to work.

Of course, there are still all sorts of magic creams sporting the latest anti-aging formula dreamed up by the high-tech cosmetic research laboratories. Yet, people increasingly seem to feel that it makes no sense to put synthetic chemicals on our skin and hair when we could be using beauty therapies drawn from natural, organic sources that are better for both the earth and ourselves. We still know so little about the healing properties of plants that it seems absurd to invent synthetic chemical answers to problems like dry skin or dull hair when a much more effective solution could already be growing in our gardens.

looking good the organic way

The important elements in looking your best are glowing skin and hair, bright eyes, well-tended hands and feet, and healthy teeth. A balanced diet of fresh, preferably organic food is the first step toward achieving all of these: Your skin and hair need plenty of vitamins and minerals (see "We Are What We Eat" on page 30). However, there is nothing wrong with enhancing your natural assets, and one of the best ways of doing that is by using some of the many beauty products that contain healthy, organically produced ingredients.

Organic beauty products are becoming more and more popular. Some of the manufacturers are still literally cottage industries, but other brands are no longer regarded as niche products. Jurlique and Dr. Hauschka produce skin-care systems made from organic ingredients that base their appeal on their purity and are doing very well indeed. Jurlique products—made on a biodynamic farm in Australia—have become quite popular since actress Nicole Kidman announced that she went nowhere without their moisturizer, while the Dr. Hauschka range is more affordable and gaining in popularity, especially among young European women. Products like these are increasingly available all over the world and can be bought through outlets such as pharmacies, health-food stores, beauty salons, and the Internet.

There are also plenty of natural treatments that you can make yourself using herbs you have grown in your organic garden or simple ingredients that are already in your kitchen. You can make a cleansing facial mask with sea salt and yogurt or avocado and mango, rinse your face with a toner made from an infusion of fresh herbs, soften your hands with a paste of almonds and rose water, or brighten your eyes with a revitalizing cold compress of cornflower and plantain. You'll find recipes for organic beauty treatments on the following pages.

There is an ever-growing number of organic beauty products on the market that benefit your body while enhancing your natural looks.

healthy hair

It is no secret that you feel your best when your hair looks good. Because it's the fastest-growing protein in the body, hair quickly reflects your general state of health. Alcohol, drugs, and depression all take a toll on your hair; enjoying a healthier diet or getting more exercise will show up there, too.

Eat plenty of sesame seeds: They are high in minerals such as iron and zinc and the antioxidant vitamin E, and are wonderful nourishment for the hair. Nettles are also rich in the minerals hair needs for healthy growth, and they make a great rinse for your hair, too. Try steaming young nettle tops (they shrink like spinach, so measure quantities accordingly), eating them with a pat of butter and a little nutmeg, and save the cooking water to use on your scalp. Onions are a wonderful source of sulfur, another mineral that is essential for healthy hair. Other sulfur-rich foods to include in your diet are watercress, cabbage, broccoli, and radishes.

External care can also make a difference to the hair's overall appearance, and it starts with the scalp. Stimulating the scalp dilates the tiny capillary blood vessels in the skin and increases the rate of blood flow to the hair follicles, thereby carrying more nutrient substances to the hair root. Better-nourished hair is healthier hair in every respect.

Many of the herbs traditionally used in hair care stimulate local circulation. Rosemary is a good example, and it's readily available. Jojoba oil, available at most good health-food stores and pharmacies, adds a wonderful luster and makes one of the best conditioning treatments. Ginger root and sesame oil are also very stimulating conditioners. Essential oils (also available from pharmacies and health-food stores) also crop up in natural hair treatments: Geranium, tea tree, and lavender have all been found to be excellent.

Steamed young nettle tops taste like spinach and are full of minerals that promote healthy hair growth.

HAIR TREATMENTS

★ To stimulate the scalp, add a handful of fresh rosemary sprigs to cold water, simmer for 15 minutes, then swab the roots of your hair with the liquid before shampooing. Or rub a raw onion into the roots before shampooing.

★ To condition, heat a couple of tablespoons of jojoba oil and apply to the roots of your hair before combing through. Wrap a warm towel around your head and leave on for 30 minutes before washing the oil out with a very mild shampoo. Or use a garlic press to squeeze a piece of fresh ginger root until you have produced enough juice to cover your hair (a tablespoon or more). Mix with an equal amount of sesame oil and massage through your hair and into your scalp. Wrap your head in a warm towel and leave the mixture on for as long as possible before shampooing out.

★ To make a cleanser and toner, rub the juice of steamed young nettle tops into your scalp.

★ To give your hair a boost, add 10 drops of bergamot, geranium, rosemary, or lavender oil to a miniature bottle of vodka, shake well, and rub into your scalp occasionally.

★ For dandruff and other scalp problems, add a few drops of tea tree oil to your shampoo.

★ If your children have nits or lice, combine 25 drops each of rosemary and lavender oil with 12 drops of eucalyptus and 13 drops of geranium into about 2½ ounces of almond oil and comb into their hair. Wrap plastic wrap around the hair and leave for a couple of hours. Then, shampoo and use a fine comb to remove the dead nits. Repeat, if necessary, a couple of weeks later.

glowing skin

Having healthy, smooth, glowing skin is within everyone's reach. All it takes is a good diet, plenty of exercise, and some simple lotions.

The first and best thing you can do for your skin is to eat plenty of bright red, yellow, orange, and green organic fruits and vegetables, such as apricots, peppers, carrots, strawberries, tomatoes, and broccoli. They are all rich in the carotenoids which your body converts to vitamin A—vital for healthy skin. Sesame, sunflower, and pumpkin seeds are rich in zinc. Oily fish such as sardines and mackerel provide essential fatty acids—the naturally occurring fats and oils that are good for the heart.

For external use, the best-known organic skin-care products are available internationally. Look for products that include ingredients such as green tea, grape seeds, pine bark, and turmeric because these ingredients contain oligomeric proanthocyanidins (OPCs). OPCs are naturally

Carrots are an excellent source of beta-carotene, which is converted to vitamin A in the body.

derived antioxidants that are said to help fight off lines, wrinkles, and other signs of aging.

While over-the-counter organic beauty products are generally more expensive than synthetic-based products, organic beauty treatments do not have to be expensive. For instance, gently brushing the skin with wet or dry coarse material such as a loofah, a roughly woven towel, or a soft brush removes dead skin and avoids the need for abrasive body scrubs, which can damage the delicate new skin underneath.

Three herbs that turn up over and over again in natural skin-care regimes—comfrey, calendula, and chamomile—have unique powers to soften, soothe, protect, and heal the skin and can easily be grown in your garden. Comfrey promotes the growth and regeneration of skin tissue, calendula clears up infection—fungal, viral, or bacterial—and counters inflammation, while chamomile soothes, heals, and stimulates cell regeneration.

Be kind to your skin and the environment by gently washing with olive oil soap rather than with harsh synthetic soaps and body scrubs.

Give yourself a facial sauna using fresh herbs (see "Skin Treatments" on page 77). Lavender repairs and soothes skin; rosemary and calendula are healing; rosemary also stimulates circulation; cornflower is refreshing; calendula, and sage are good for blemishes and minor infections; and comfrey and borage flowers are great for dry skin. Thyme will open your pores and really get your blood pumping.

Many natural skin-care products contain almond oil. You can make your own treatment by adding a few drops of your favorite essential oil to a bottle of almond oil. If you have oily skin, chamomile, lavender, or rose will be most useful, while neroli (citrus blossom) or clary sage are good for older skins. Twice a week, put the oil on your face and leave for 20 minutes before washing it off with warm water and applying a toner to close the pores and tighten the skin. Some herbal teas make good facial toners, too: Peppermint is wonderful for oily skin, chamomile calms puffy or reddened skin, and lime flower revitalizes the skin and soothes sunburn. Store unused toner in the refrigerator for up to a week.

above: *The flesh of a mango puréed with an avocado makes a nourshing face mask.*
right: *Sea salt added to a carton of natural live yogurt and massaged well into your face is a simple, inexpensive, yet effective exfoliant and cleanser.*

SKIN TREATMENTS

★ For a wonderful facial rinse, make a strong infusion of comfrey, calendula, and chamomile, using a total of 1 ounce of dried herbs (or 1½ ounces fresh) in 2 cups of boiling water. Cover and let stand for at least 10 minutes, then strain. This mixture can also be added to your bath to scent the water.

★ To make a facial toner for use after cleansing, steep fresh lavender tops in white wine vinegar for a week (shake the bottle occasionally), then dilute it with 4 parts water to 1 part vinegar.

★ To give yourself a facial sauna, put a handful of fresh herbs as appropriate (see page 76) into a pan and pour boiling water on top. Cover and let infuse for 10 minutes, then heat to almost boiling. Remove the pan from the heat and lean over it with a towel over your head for no more than 5 minutes.

★ To make a cleansing facial mask, purée the pulp of a whole orange and apply it to your skin for 20 minutes, then rinse off with tepid water.

★ For an exfoliating cleansing mask, add 2 teaspoons of sea salt to a carton of live yogurt. (Check the label to make sure it contains live cultures.) Stir the mixture well and smooth over your face, massaging it in with your fingertips. Let the mask dry for 30 minutes, then rinse off with tepid water. Splash cold water onto your face to finish.

★ For a nourishing face mask, purée together the pulp of a mango and an avocado. Apply generously and leave on for 15 minutes, then remove with a soft cotton cloth and rinse your face with warm water.

bright eyes

Take some time to give your eyes a treat as part of your beauty routine. Compresses are one of the best ways to keep your eyes bright. To make a compress, add some eye lotion (see below) to ice-cold water, soak a cotton pad in the solution, and apply one to each eye.

Eye lotions often contain eyebright, an herb that seems to soothe and counter inflammation. Eyebright is also available as eye drops. Witch hazel is another common ingredient of natural eye lotions because it is so marvelously soothing. Lotions can be applied sparingly above and below the eye, but avoid getting them in the eye.

fresh mouth, strong teeth, healthy gums

Dentistry may not seem to fall under the realm of organic self-treatment, but there are plenty of natural ways to get your mouth in good condition. Tea tree toothpaste, for

left: *An infusion made from dried cornflowers, eyebright, and plantain leaves makes a good cold compress for tired eyes.*
following pages: *A mixture of rose water—an infusion made from rose petals—and glycerine makes an excellent hand moisturizer.*

example, is one of the best antiseptics—good for teeth and breath. The taste is strong, but if you persevere, you'll eventually get used to it.

Propolis is a sticky, resinous substance gathered by bees, and it has remarkable antibiotic qualities—it is by far and away the best treatment I know for mouth ulcers—and has been used as a healing agent for thousands of years. It is generally effective for any infections of the mouth or throat. You can find it in most good health-food stores.

Certain herbs are more prevalent than others in natural toothpastes: horsetail, which contains silica (a mineral that is vital for healthy teeth); echinacea, which fights infections; myrrh, which is very useful for gum infections; and sage, which stimulates the mucous membranes and the gums. In the Middle Ages, women used to rub fresh sage leaves on their teeth to make them whiter and improve their gums. Follow their example and put a sage plant in your window box.

To counter bad breath, chew mint leaves, parsley, tarragon, or fennel—all of which can be grown organically in your own garden or in pots on your windowsill. Or chew cardamom pods or cumin seeds to clear your palate.

EYE TREATMENTS

★ To make a cold compress, mix 5 ounces (140 grams) of eyebright and 1 ounce (25 grams) each of cornflowers and plantain leaves. Pour 3½ ounces of boiling water over a tablespoonful of this mixture and let it infuse for 30 minutes. Then strain and cool, and apply as a cold compress to bring your eyes back to life. You can substitute chamomile or calendula for the eyebright.

★ To rejuvenate your eyes, grate or slice a potato very finely and lay it across the eyes.

MOUTH TREATMENTS

★ For an effective mouth disinfectant, add 3 to 4 drops of tincture of myrrh (which you can find in health-food stores) to a glass of water. Be prepared: It is very bitter.

★ To make a tea tree mouthwash, add 3 to 4 drops of tea tree oil to 6 ounces of water and swish gently around your mouth before spitting out.

★ Make your own sage or horsetail toothpowder by crushing 2 teaspoons of fresh leaves in a pestle and mortar and putting them in a small ovenproof dish with a tablespoon of sea salt. Put the dish in a warm oven until the leaves are crisp and dry, and then grind them to a powder. Make a batch and keep it in an airtight container.

soft hands and feet

Hands are endlessly exposed to harsh treatment: Dishwashing liquid, soaps, shampoos, and household cleaners are all possible irritants and can result in very dry skin.

Most natural hand products are based on almond oil, which is wonderful for reddened or chafed skin. Rose water used by itself can be drying; however, it helps keep in moisture when added to other creams or liquids. Mix equal parts of rose water and glycerine (both available in pharmacies) and together they will stop moisture evaporating from your skin. Before bed, rub some essential oils into your hands (see below).

If your poor, tired feet are a bit sweaty, put a few drops of peppermint oil into a tepid footbath—this will stop them from aching, too. Tea tree oil can also help with this problem, as well as with fungal infections. A piece of pumice stone will gently rub away rough skin.

Use a piece of pumice stone to gently rub away the rough skin on your feet while relaxing in the bath.

HAND TREATMENTS

★ If your hands feel rough, make a soft paste of ground almonds and a little rose water and spread it on your hands like a facial mask. Rinse off and smooth in some hand cream afterward and your skin will feel great.

★ If your hands are dry, mix 2 ounces of almond oil with about 25 drops of chamomile, lavender, or benzoin oil in a glass bottle, then add the contents of a vitamin E capsule. Before going to bed, warm the bottle under a hot tap, massage the oil into your hands, and sleep tight.

★ To strengthen nails, add 1 tablespoon of dried horsetail to 1½ cups of boiling water and leave to infuse for half an hour before soaking your nails in the liquid.

exercise your body, mind, and spirit

Regular physical activity is vital for both health and beauty, and nothing could be more organic than using your own body to keep itself fit and healthy. Working the cardiovascular system improves the functioning of the heart and lungs and dramatically reduces the risk of heart disease. By maintaining muscle strength, you also maintain joint function, which is especially important if you already suffer from arthritis. Fitness is a combination of strength, stamina, and mobility, so whatever exercise you choose, it should combine all three of these factors for maximum benefit.

Regular exercise also has a beneficial effect on the peripheral circulation that supplies blood to the skin. With this increased blood flow comes the delivery of extra nutrients and the removal of waste products, a combination that produces healthy, glowing skin. In my health practice, I have often observed that people who exercise regularly generally tend to adopt healthier lifestyles, so they are less likely to smoke or drink excessive amounts of alcohol and are much more likely to be eating a sensible and healthy diet—all contributors to overall beauty and well-being.

left: Setting aside a few minutes each day for some simple meditation will help you feel more relaxed.
following pages: Swimming can be one of the most effective and enjoyable aerobic exercises. Set the pace that suits your fitness level and your mood.

These days, no one—from the factory floor to the boardroom—is immune to stress. Stress affects our looks and, more importantly, our health—over time, it can lead to potentially fatal disorders. Exercise is one of the best ways of dealing with stress. Regular activity such as playing a sport you enjoy will take your mind off your worries and ensure a constant supply of endorphins, the body's feel-good hormones. And when you've finished your workout, complete the destressing process with a simple 15-minute relaxation technique (see "Meditation: Instant Nirvana" on this page).

It is never too late to start exercising, although the older you are and the less active you have been throughout your life, the more care you must take (see "From Fat to Fit" on page 86). If you are out of condition, start gradually. Yoga is a good way to start stretching and mobilizing muscles and joints.

Aerobic exercise is the key to heart protection and great skin, as it has the greatest and the most prolonged effect on the circulatory system. Aerobic exercises involve sustained exertion that increases the body's ability to deliver oxygenated blood to the skin, muscles, and organs. Such exercises can include circuit training or aerobic classes in your local gym, or individual activities such as running, jogging, swimming, cycling, rowing, cross-country skiing, brisk walking, or even skipping.

Any continuous physical activity that increases your breathing rate and the speed of your heartbeat is aerobic.

(continued on page 88)

MEDITATION: INSTANT NIRVANA

Promoting inner peace helps overcome stress and anxiety. Going to regular yoga or meditation classes is great, but you could start with this simple 15-minute meditation plan. First, turn off the television, radio, and telephone, then sit or lie comfortably. Shut your eyes. Relax your muscles by stretching left and right arms alternately along the sides of your body five times, holding for 10 seconds and relaxing. Repeat once with both arms at the same time. Take five deep breaths. Repeat with legs, then arms and legs at the same time. Breathe deeply through your nose and repeat the word "one" continuously for 10 minutes, pushing all other thoughts out of your mind. Rest with eyes shut for 2 minutes before getting up.

FROM FAT TO FIT

Before starting any exercise program, you must assess your own fitness. If you are overweight and over 40 and have hardly moved a muscle since you left school, seek professional advice before you start. To help you decide where you stand, answer the following questions truthfully, then add up your score. Each "yes" answer equals one point.

1. Are you over 40 years old?
2. Has it been more than 5 years since you've exercised on a regular basis?
3. Do you regularly go home and spend the evening asleep in front of the television?
4. Do you have any joint disease or deformity?
5. Are you more than 15 pounds overweight?
6. Do you ever become dizzy or faint?
7. Do you smoke?
8. Do you feel ill or uncomfortable after running to catch the train or bus?
9. Do you get out of breath easily?
10. Do you have problems sleeping?
11. Have you ever had a serious back problem?
12. Do you drink more than three alcoholic beverages a day?

0–3 Good: Start exercising today.
3–6 Just in time: Start gently and persevere.
6–12 You may not make it to the gym! Get some advice before you start.

Note: If you have ever been told that you have high blood pressure or heart disease, you can exercise, but you must seek professional advice before you start.

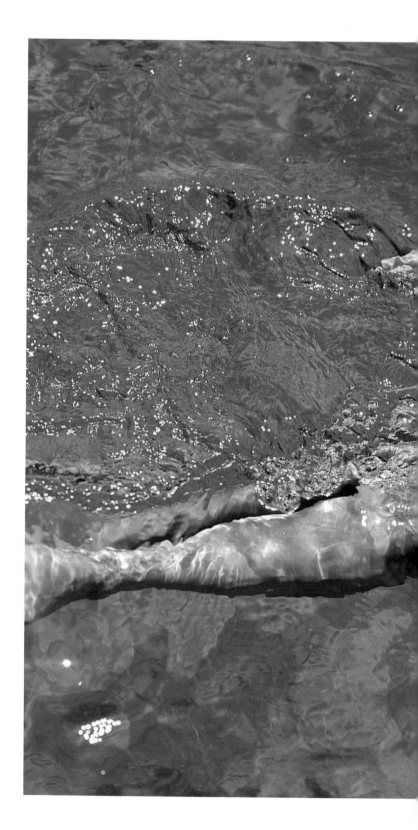

Raking leaves, sawing logs, shoveling snow, and doing energetic housework all provide your body with a form of aerobic exercise. If you are not reasonably fit, you can't supply sufficient oxygen to your muscles to maintain physical exertion, and you will be breathless after swimming one length of the pool or climbing a short flight of stairs. You'll know you are on the right track when you can push your heart rate up and keep working at the appropriate level for at least 15 minutes (see "Training Levels," on this page).

Long-term fitness is achieved by regular aerobic exercise. Aim to burn around 2,000 calories per week, and choose exercises or sports (preferably both) that suit you. If you enjoy what you're doing, your exercise sessions won't be a chore. Take your build, natural ability, temperament, and lifestyle into account, and choose appropriate activities that will fit into your normal routine.

It's important to start gently and build up gradually, and always warm up before exercise and cool down afterward. Follow the "Safety First" instructions on this page and you won't go wrong.

TRAINING LEVELS

Most adults have a resting pulse of 60 to 80 beats per minute. Find your pulse rate (the number of times your heart beats in 1 minute) by pressing your wrist on the thumb side; count the beats for 15 seconds, then multiply by 4 to find the rate per minute. Aerobic sport or exercise should raise your pulse from its normal rate to more than 100 beats per minute.

Recommended heart rates per minute for best aerobic effort:

Age	Heart rate	Age	Heart rate
20	138–158	55	127–146
25	137–156	60	126–144
30	135–154	65	125–142
35	134–153	70	123–141
40	132–151	75	122–139
45	131–150	80	120–138
50	129–147	85	119–136

safety first

No strenuous aerobic exercise or sport should be undertaken by any person who is not already reasonably fit. This is because your heart can react abnormally if it's launched into sudden action. Many of the movements involved in aerobics can sprain or tear muscles, tendons, and ligaments if your body is unused to exercise, so build up to aerobic exercises gently.

★ Don't exercise if you have a fever or viral infection. Not only will these conditions affect your performance, but your muscles, joints, heart, or respiratory system may become inflamed and your general condition may worsen.

★ Don't exercise if you feel dizzy, faint, out of breath, or sick. If symptoms persist, consult a medical practitioner.

★ If exercise is really painful, stop. Start again after a day or two with gentle stretching exercises.

★ Train, don't strain. Build up gradually to your chosen exercise. Be patient and don't overdo things. It may take several weeks before you feel the benefits of exercise.

★ Always warm up and cool down before and after exercise in order to regulate the heart rate and to stretch and relax muscles to reduce the risk of stiffness and injury. Use gentle movements such as swinging your arms, stretching your legs, and bending your knees.

★ After cooling down, relax your tired muscles in a warm bath or shower.

★ Never exercise immediately after eating. In order to avoid a stomachache or cramps, wait at least 2 hours after eating before exercising.

★ Never exercise in really hot weather. It is debilitating and you could become dehydrated.

EXERCISES

As an osteopath, I've devised this set of exercises for my patients. Though originally designed to help with back problems, they are ideal for maintaining strength and mobility of the abdominal muscles, neck and shoulder region, and the rest of the spine.

Spend 10 minutes 3 times a week and choose 10 exercises for each session, making sure that you vary them from week to week. Good muscle tone not only protects you against injury and joint damage but also contributes to good skin tone, a key factor in any beauty regime.

1 ★ THE TAIL TUCK

position: Lying on back, knees bent, feet flat on floor.

exercise: Flatten the hollow of your back on the floor, using your abdominal muscles to pull the abdomen down. Raise your pelvis just off the floor, but do not lift your lower back. Hold for 5 seconds. Relax pelvis for 5 seconds but keep your back flat on the floor. Repeat 5 times, keeping your breathing regular throughout the exercise.

2 ★ THE STRAIGHT LEG TAIL TUCK

position: Lying on back, knees bent, feet flat on floor.

exercise: Flatten the hollow of your back on the floor, using your abdominal muscles to pull the abdomen down. Gradually straighten both legs, keeping your back pressed to the floor, then bend your legs again. Repeat 5 times. This prepares you for the standing tail tuck (exercise 3).

3 ★ THE STANDING TAIL TUCK

position: Standing, back against a wall, feet 6 to 8 inches away from the baseboard.

exercise: Flatten the small of your back against the wall using your abdominal muscles. Do not bend your knees. Hold for 5 seconds. Relax and repeat 5 times. Keep breathing regularly throughout. You can practice this against an imaginary wall at any time while standing.

4 ★ THE SKIER'S TAIL TUCK

position: Standing, back against a wall, feet 6 to 8 inches away from the baseboard.

exercise: Flatten the small of your back against the wall using your abdominal muscles, as in exercise 3, but slowly bend your knees, keeping your back flat against the wall. Hold for 15 seconds. Repeat 3 times with 5-second rests in between. Do not let your flattened back come away from the wall. As you get better at this exercise, increase the amount you bend your knees until they reach a 90-degree angle, as though you are sitting on a chair. Continue until you can hold this position for a full minute.

5 ★ THE BUTT SQUEEZE

position: Standing, the cheeks of your buttocks squeezed firmly together.

exercise: Flatten the small of your back. Squeezing your buttocks together, walk around the room for 1 minute.

6 ★ THE HEAD-UP

position: Lying on back, knees bent, feet flat on floor.

exercise: Flatten your back on the floor, arms up, with fingers pointing toward the ceiling, chin on chest. Roll forward until your shoulder blades are off the floor. Hold for 5 seconds. Roll back to floor, keeping your tailbone tucked in. Build up to 10 repetitions.

7 ★ THE SIT-DOWN

position: Sitting on floor, knees bent, arms around knees.

exercise: Lean backward slowly, using your arms to support the weight of your torso. Use your arm muscles to pull back into the sitting position. Rest for 5 seconds. Repeat 10 times. As your abdominal muscles gain in strength, you can reduce the strength used by the hands and arms until you can perform the exercise 10 times without holding your knees. You can then move on to the sit-up with toe touch (exercise 8).

(continued)

EXERCISES—CONTINUED

8 ★ THE SIT-UP WITH TOE TOUCH

Be sure you're proficient at exercise 7 before you consider this exercise.

position: Flat on back, knees bent, feet flat on floor.

exercise: Tuck in your bottom and, with chin on chest and hands along your sides, roll upright from the neck, keeping your tail tucked. When sitting upright, straighten your legs, stretch your fingers to toes, then roll slowly back to floor, bending your knees. Work up to 10 repetitions.

9 ★ THE ONE HAMSTRING PROTECTED STRETCH

Hamstrings are the large muscles at the back of the thighs. Loss of elasticity in these muscles inhibits bending and correct spinal movement. Stretching both hamstrings at once is counterproductive since it can do harm and trigger pain without any appreciable benefit.

position: Sitting on floor, one knee fully bent and foot flat on the floor; other leg extended.

exercise: Allow the bent knee to fall outward, and stretch both hands toward the foot of your straight leg as far as comfortable. Now start a gentle, rhythmic, bouncing movement, reaching for the foot. Continue for 20 seconds. Rest, change legs, and repeat.

10 ★ AWAY WITH ACHILLES HEEL

Shortened Achilles tendons impede walking and limit how much your knees can bend when you are bending or lifting. They play an important part in the cause of chronic back pain. These tendons may be stretched while doing exercise 9 by placing the foot of your straight leg flat against a wall and maintaining this contact during the exercise. Alternatively:

position: Standing 2 to 3 feet from a wall, leaning toward wall with palms flat against it, both feet on the ground.

exercise: Move one foot half the distance to the wall

Keep your other leg straight at the knee, with your heel flat on the floor. Now, bend the forward knee and both arms slowly and rhythmically. Keep the back heel on the floor and your butt tucked in at all times. Continue for 20 seconds. Relax. Change legs and repeat 10 times.

11 ★ THE ONE LEG UP

position: Lying on back, one leg bent with foot flat on the floor, other leg straight, butt tucked in.

exercise: Without bending the knee of the straight leg, raise it upward until it is level with the knee of the bent leg. Hold for 5 seconds, lower slowly, then rest for 5 seconds. Repeat 5 times, change legs, and do 5 more lifts with the other leg.

12 ★ THE TWO LEGS UP

Until you are several weeks into your exercise plan, stick with the one leg up (exercise 11). Lifting the weight of both legs off the floor at the same time places a severe strain on the lower lumbar joints. Unless you already have excellent muscle control, it will inevitably increase the curve in your lower back and may induce pain.

position: Lying flat on floor, heels resting on a chair seat, legs raised to an angle of at least 30 degrees, butt tucked in. By maintaining this position, you will avoid increasing your lumbar curve.

exercise: Keeping both knees straight, raise both legs to 90 degrees and lower them slowly. Rest for 5 seconds. Build up to 10 repetitions.

13 ★ THE CROSSOVER LEG PRESS

This isometric exercise, which uses the strength of two groups of muscles pitted against each other, really strengthens the abdominal muscles without movement.

position: Lying on back, both knees bent, feet flat on floor, butt tucked in.

exercise: Raise your right knee until the calf is parallel to the floor and you can place your outstretched left hand on the right knee, keeping your arm straight. Raise your head and tuck your chin into your chest. Push your hand against your knee and knee against hand, using the muscle strength of your shoulder and arm against that of your knee and hip; this creates a powerful action of the abdominal muscles. Hold this pressure for 5 seconds and relax. Repeat 5 times, then switch to other hand and leg for 5 repetitions.

14 ★ THE CROSSOVER SIT-UP

position: Flat on back, legs straight, butt tucked in, legs spread legs apart to 45 degrees.

exercise: Tuck your chin into your chest and place your right arm across your body. Pushing your right shoulder toward your left leg, raise your torso until both shoulder blades are off the floor. Relax and repeat 5 times. Change arms and stretch left shoulder to right leg. Repeat 5 times.

The next six exercises are for strengthening and relaxing the neck muscles. Whether your original problem is at the top or bottom of your back makes no difference. The spine is one unit; although it is made up of many different parts, a problem with any section of the vertebral column affects how the entire unit functions.

15 ★ THE CHIN-UP

The chin-up is an isometric exercise and requires no movement. Do not exert so much pressure that your neck muscles start to tremble since this will cause irritation of the muscle tissues.

position: Sitting.

exercise: Clasp fingers of both hands together and place behind your head. Try to tilt your chin upward while pushing against your head for 10 seconds. Repeat 5 times.

16 ★ THE CHIN-DOWN

position: Sitting.

exercise: Place the palms of both hands firmly against your forehead and press your head against your hands, trying to push your chin down toward your chest. Hold for 10 seconds. Repeat 5 times.

17 ★ EAR TO SHOULDER

position: Sitting.

exercise: Try to move your head sideways—your left ear toward your left shoulder—while pushing with your hand against the side of your head. Hold this position for 10 seconds. Repeat 5 times. Relax, then repeat the exercise with your right hand on the right side of your head. Do 5 repetitions.

18 ★ THE SHOULDER DROP

position: Sitting or standing.

exercise: Raise your shoulders as high as possible while keeping your arms by your sides. Hold this position for 5 seconds, then allow your shoulders to drop with their own weight. Repeat 3 times.

19 ★ CHEST OUT

position: Sitting or standing.

exercise: Push both shoulders back as far as possible, sticking out your chest and forcing your shoulder blades together. Hold this position for 5 seconds. Relax and repeat 3 times.

20 ★ CHEST IN

position: Sitting or standing.

exercise: Push both shoulders forward as far as possible, narrowing your chest and forcing your shoulder blades as far apart as possible, keeping your arms by your sides. Hold this position for 5 seconds. Relax and repeat three times. Hold for 5 seconds. Relax and repeat 3 times.

natural remedies and health therapies

The organic movement and natural complementary therapies have always seemed inseparable to me. As a practitioner, I see no sense in advising patients to eat healthy organic food, yet at the same time increasing the toxic load of chemicals to which they and their families are subjected. No one can deny the benefits of the pharmaceutical industry—the development of lifesaving drugs and powerful analgesics, the ongoing battle to find cures for terminal diseases—but the excessive use of many of these drugs puts the delicately balanced ecosystem of both the planet and the human body at risk. Complementary therapies, by contrast, are part of a gentle medicine that has a very low impact on our environment.

The rise in popularity of herbal remedies has also given organic agriculture a boost, as manufacturers often use organic raw materials in their products. Many plants used in herbal medicine originate from the Amazonian rain forests—another reason why its important to protect these and other endangered regions.

With this benefit in mind, it makes sense to consider natural therapies as part of organic living—but it is important to make sure you have an accurate diagnosis before embarking on any form of self-medication or trying complementary therapies. Discuss your health concerns, as well as any alternative medicines or treatments you may wish to try, with your regular doctor. Never take any medication during pregnancy without first consulting your doctor.

naturopathy

Naturopathy is the term for a drugless approach to medicine based on the principle that the body can heal itself. Instead of trying to treat specific diseases, the practitioner focuses on encouraging the healing process and avoiding anything that might interfere with it. Fresh air, sunlight, exercise, rest, good nutrition, relaxation, hydrotherapy (water treatments), manual manipulation of the spine or other joints, and other techniques are all part of the naturopath's medicine chest. Naturopathy is the original holistic therapy, aiming to treat the patient, not just the symptoms.

In many respects, the naturopath can be seen as an alternative general practitioner, and often a combination of

Lots of fresh air and sunshine are two of the key elements in naturopathic healing.

HYDROTHERAPY

★ You don't have to visit a spa to benefit from hydrotherapy: The main ingredient is on tap in your bathroom, and everything else is available in your nearest pharmacy.

★ A cold bath is highly invigorating and leaves your skin with a warm, healthy glow. Sit in a bath filled with 6 inches of cold water and give your body a good splash for 1 minute. Kneel, add another 6 inches of water, and repeat the splashing. Then finish by briefly lying down in the cold water.

★ For backache or chest problems, add 2 tablespoons of bath mustard to a hot bath. Add chamomile, seaweed, or peat extracts for the skin; hop oil for tension and insomnia; or Epsom salts for arthritis or rheumatism.

★ If you're feeling anxious or depressed, throw a few herbal tea bags into the bath. Lime blossom, chamomile, or valerian are the best for improving your mood.

★ Alternate hot and cold water to stimulate circulation. In cases of varicose veins, hemorrhoids, swelling due to overexposure to cold, or muscle, joint, or ligament injuries, soak the affected body part in hot water containing 10 drops of rosemary oil per gallon for 3 minutes, then in cold water for 30 seconds. Repeat at least 5 times, twice a day, ending with cold water.

orthodox and naturopathic therapies produces the best possible outcome for the patient. Few mainstream doctors would object to patients with high blood pressure seeking advice on stress reduction, improved diet, and relaxation techniques from a naturopath, while at the same time continuing to take their blood-pressure medication.

herbal medicine

The use of medicinal herbs has a long and well-documented history worldwide. For thousands of years, herbalism was the usual system of healing, and many of the drugs prescribed by conventional doctors contain ingredients derived from herbs familiar to herbalists. Digoxin, morphine, codeine, ephedrine, and taxol are just some of the medicines in use everyday that are derived from plants.

The herbalist uses medicines made from the plant itself, so that every constituent in the original plant is found in the herbal remedy. By contrast, modern medicine extracts only the single active ingredient from a plant, or synthesizes it in the laboratory, and uses it in isolation. The herbalist believes that such extraction could eliminate vital ingredients that aid the healing process in undiscovered ways.

Herbal medicines can be used to treat a wide range of physical and nervous disorders, and some herbal remedies are accessible to almost everyone (although you should always consult your health care practitioner before treating yourself, or if you are pregnant, as some herbs can be dangerous in certain circumstances). The regular use of herbal teas and infusions can promote good health. For example, drinking a hot infusion of elderflower and peppermint during the first hours of a cold or flu can disperse the infection.

Depression, anxiety, and insomnia can all be helped by herbal remedies that have a gentle sedative action on the nervous system, such as valerian, vervain, lemon balm, and St. John's wort. These herbs let patients avoid the hazards of

dependency and withdrawal symptoms. (Note, however, that St. John's wort may interact with blood-thinning drugs such as Warfarin, and should not be taken by anyone receiving immunosuppressant therapy following transplant surgery or treatment for HIV and AIDS.)

homeopathy

Homeopathy is a system of medicine based on the healing power of nature. Homeopathy means literally "like disease" and works on the principle of "let like be cured by like." Homeopathy stimulates the body to heal itself. The patient is treated with a minute dose of medication that would cause the symptoms of the illness if it were taken in large doses by a healthy person. Remedies are prepared by a process of dilution, on the principle that the greater the dilution, the more powerful the remedy.

When you're being treated by a homeopath, expect him or her to spend a lot of time questioning you about factors that make your problem better or worse, such as the time of day, the season, or the weather. The remedy your homeopath chooses will closely match your total requirements; there is no standard medicine for specific complaints, and the cure is tailor-made for each patient. Because it is based on the patient's symptoms, homeopathy can be applied in almost any medical situation.

Available as pill, powder, or liquid, homeopathic remedies are considered safe enough that 95 percent of them are sold over the counter in the United States in many health-food stores, according to the National Center for Homeopathy. Always keep them in a cool, dark place in an airtight container away from strong-smelling substances such as disinfectants. Many practitioners advise avoiding coffee, mint, and alcohol during treatment. If self-treatment

The healing qualities of garlic have been well known to herbalists for centuries. Eat fresh raw garlic each day, and you will be less likely to suffer from colds.

hasn't worked after a reasonable number of doses, consult a homeopathic practitioner.

acupuncture

Acupuncture is the best-researched of all the complementary therapies and, worldwide, it's used by far more people than conventional Western medicine. Acupuncture is an effective form of pain relief and can also be used to treat most illnesses, especially migraines, digestive problems, sinus problems, rheumatism, arthritis, skin disorders, and irregular periods.

This traditional Chinese system of medicine uses small needles inserted into precise points on the body to rebalance its flow of energy, or *chi*. It is believed that chi flows through the body in pathways known as "meridians," which each relate to a specific organ or function. The acupuncture points lie along the meridians and may be nowhere near the organ concerned. For extra stimulation, heat or electricity can be applied to the needles; treatment is mostly pain free.

acupressure

Acupressure, the technique of applying pressure to acupuncture points, rather than using needles, is a common form of family first aid in China. Acupressure is used mainly to reduce stress. Acupressure is the older of the two techniques, a Chinese home remedy that gave rise to acupuncture. Its goal is the same as that of acupuncture: to stimulate chi. But instead of using needles, it uses finger or hand pressure along the meridians. One main benefit of acupressure is that you can do it yourself once you've learned the basics. And it's simple, safe, and free.

reflexology

Reflexology is the practice of applying pressure to very precise points on the feet. The principles of this therapy are similar to acupuncture; the reflexologist aims to redirect flows of bodily energy from the "reflex areas" in the feet into organs or structures that are either deficient or overactive.

Practitioners claim to be able to diagnose through reflexology. While there is not much evidence to support this claim and any suggested diagnosis should be confirmed by your family doctor, the therapy is extremely popular and many people seem to benefit from it. It is often used to treat migraines, skin problems, digestive disorders, stress-related conditions, and allergies.

chiropractic

According to the International Chiropractors Association, chiropractic is the fastest-growing and second-largest type of primary health care, with more than 60,000 doctors of chiropractic in the United States. Chiropractors practice treatment based on the manipulation of bones or other parts of the body, not just the back, as is often assumed.

Manipulative treatment helps maintain and repair the mechanical structures of the body and is noninvasive, unlike drug treatments and surgery. Specific manipulations are used to restore the bones, joints, ligaments, tendons, and muscles to working order wherever possible. Most people visit chiropractors for back problems and many physicians and orthopedic surgeons support this approach. However, you should be aware that some back conditions are not suitable for chiropractic treatment.

Neck and shoulder pain, sports injuries, migraine, arthritis, asthma, digestive disorders, postural problems, and even menstrual cramps can all be helped. Chiropractic is particularly useful during and after pregnancy, as it helps maintain good posture and compensates for the gradual loosening of pelvic ligaments.

the alexander technique

In this technique, the human body is viewed as a complex piece of engineering thrown out of balance by bad physical habits, such as slouching or other types of poor posture. Constant repetition from a very young age makes these bad habits feel "right," but the result is the malfunction of the whole system. By retraining posture and movement and replacing the bad habits with a set of positive ones, the Alexander Technique has far-reaching, positive effects on both mental and physical health.

The key to this practice is the relationship between the head, neck, and back, and a teacher of this technique will focus on making you more aware of these relationships.

Getting real benefit from this technique means lots of homework. You will need to spend 15 to 30 minutes every day practicing what you have been taught, but it is well worth the effort in terms of health improvement. Complaints caused by excess tension in the body, such as high blood pressure, asthma, irritable bowel syndrome, headaches, backache, and even repetitive strain injury can all benefit from improved posture and a reduction in stress. The American Association for the Alexander Technique provides a complete listing of certified teachers on its Web site (www.alexandertech.com).

hypnosis

In the hands of a trained hypnotherapist, hypnosis is a powerful tool that can treat phobias, help the patient give up smoking, reduce high blood pressure, and more. Hypnosis not only alleviates symptoms but also trains the mind (the source of the problem) to work differently. The benefits of hypnosis increase with practice, so hypnotherapists may teach the patient techniques of self-hypnosis to supplement the formal sessions.

Hypnosis can be especially valuable as a means of alternative pain control, especially for the increasing numbers of women who prefer natural childbirth. An example of using self-hypnosis to control pain comes from the Harvard Medical School. In a study of 241 patients undergoing minor surgery, one-third of the patients were taught self-hypnosis techniques to control their pain. For example, they were encouraged to visualize muscle relaxation and sensations of floating, and to practice deep breathing. Only the patients using self-hypnosis said their pain did not get worse during surgery; they also experienced less anxiety and needed less self-administered painkilling medication during the procedure.

Hypnosis isn't magic, nor is it hocus-pocus. In the right hands, it is a valuable therapy that can help people deal with their phobia or addiction, or allow them to cope more easily and naturally with the pain of serious illness.

aromatherapy

This therapy uses essential oils: highly concentrated, highly scented extracts derived from plants. Oils are either inhaled or diluted in an inert carrier oil such as grapeseed oil and then absorbed through the skin. Their effect may be physical—stimulating the nervous or respiratory systems, relieving swelling, or fighting infection—or emotional, promoting relaxation and positive feelings. During aromatherapy massage the oil works in two ways: Active ingredients are absorbed; at the same time, the fragrant vapors are inhaled.

Different oils are appropriate for different problems. Aromatherapy can be effective in raising energy levels, in relieving respiratory illnesses such as bronchitis and asthma, in soothing sports injuries, and for cases of post-operative recovery and most children's ailments. You can use aromatherapy oils at home, but see a qualified practitioner if you have medical problems or are pregnant, as some oils can be extremely dangerous in specific situations.

massage

Massage is one of the simplest, cheapest, and most rewarding of all therapies. It is easy to learn basic techniques to use on friends and family, and a massage by a professional masseur

USING ESSENTIAL OILS

★ The safest way to inhale is to sniff the air just above the oil (rather than the oil itself). You could also add a drop of oil to your pillowcase or burn a candle scented with oil—but not while you are drifting off to sleep!

★ Before applying the oil to your skin, always dilute it in grapeseed oil (5 to 6 drops of essential oil to 2 tablespoons of carrier oil), then massage the oil into your skin.

★ Add a few drops of oil to a warm bath, or mix a drop or two in warm water and soak a cloth in the water to make a compress.

★ Basil, orange, rose, and lime oils raise energy levels.

★ Eucalyptus, geranium, tea tree, and rosemary oils can reduce lower back pain.

★ Chamomile, rose, and ylang-ylang oils are effective for symptoms of premenstrual syndrome (PMS) .

★ Lemongrass, jasmine, lavender, geranium, ylang-ylang, marjoram, and bergamot oils all combat stress.

★ Lavender, peppermint, and rosemary oils are effective for headaches.

★ Eucalyptus and tea tree oils help fight cold symptoms.

is a great joy. Whether it is simply for the reduction of stress and anxiety, the easing of aching muscles after a hard day's work, remedial massage following an accident or sports injury, a comforting and supportive massage in terminal care, or a children's and baby massage to encourage good sleep, the patient will always feel better afterward—this ancient art should be on everyone's agenda as a regular mind, body, and spirit treat.

other complementary treatments

There are many other complementary therapies in practice today, some of which defy all common sense and logical explanation, and some of which may perhaps produce good results for you. I believe it is important to keep an open mind but equally important to maintain a healthy skepticism—especially where your health or the health of your family is concerned. Always consult your health-care practitioner before putting your faith into any form of complementary medicine.

Aromatherapy masseurs use specially chosen essential oils diluted in a carrier of grapeseed or almond oil.

treating the whole person

When I started my practice in the 1960s, my work was referred to as "fringe" medicine. By the end of the 1970s, it had progressed to "alternative," and then by the 1980s and 1990s it was "complementary." Today, many practitioners use the all-encompassing term "integrated" medicine.

Some patients are now being treated in a truly holistic fashion. There is a growing number of medical practices where chiropractors and rheumatologists work side by side with physiotherapists, acupuncturists, and homeopaths. There are pediatric medical centers where meditation sessions, Buddhist chanting, and color therapy go hand in hand with the high-tech skills of the neurosurgeon. You'll even find cancer centers in major university teaching hospitals where oncologists share their departments with aromatherapists and reflexologists.

All this points to a more sympathetic approach in which each individual is treated as a whole person rather than a set of symptoms. Whether you are suffering from a twisted ankle, a sports-related injury, joint disease, heart problems, or terminal illness, integrated medicine is likely to provide the best possible treatment.

... the organic home

Organic living means that we, the consumers, have to take more responsibility for the products we use; we need to have a holistic attitude toward consuming. Caring about the working conditions in which our clothes are produced is part of that attitude, as is thinking about the amount of time a new carpet will take to biodegrade when we eventually throw it away—or the effects of paint fumes on our health.

Organic living also means incorporating safe, organic products into all areas of our lives. We need to use "green" wood in construction projects; employ new technologies for harnessing wind, water, and solar power; drive less; and buy cars with the most fuel-efficient engines. We also need to use environmentally friendly cleaning products, cut down on our consumption of plastic and other synthetic materials, use products made out of recyclable glass and paper, and choose organically produced, natural fiber fabrics for furnishings as well as clothes.

Using natural materials to make simple furniture and other household objects is an important part of creating a healthy and attractive organic home.

This list of changes is a long one, but putting it into practice is easier than it looks—particularly now that the concept of organic living is becoming more popular and more organic products are being produced. Of course, some organic products may lose their individuality as larger companies become involved. Some of the smaller companies could even go out of business because they can't compete with the prices charged for products by large conglomerates.

That's why it's important that we support small producers who keep a close eye on working conditions, toxic emissions, and quality. Beautifully crafted furniture made with love and conviction, clothes woven from organic wool and cotton, fabulous toys carved from wood harvested from responsibly managed forests—all these are the work of small craftsmen. Big businesses can develop technology that will make such craftsmanship more affordable. And if the two can work together, then we will all benefit.

start with recycling

One of the most unattractive and distressing by-products of human society is the garbage dump—and the richer the country, the more garbage it produces. The United States is the largest producer of waste in the world—no other country comes close. Estimates of the amount of waste produced every year in the United States vary greatly depending on the source. The official government figure for 1998, published by the U.S. Environmental Protection Agency (EPA), was almost 1 ton per person annually; the environmental campaigners Zero Waste America (ZWA), who based their figures on data compiled by *Biocycle* magazine, suggested that the total was as much as 1.4 tons per person. ZWA has used government statistics to calculate that since 1990 the United States has disposed of more than 11 billion tons of domestic and foreign waste. This is equivalent to covering every acre in the country with nearly 4.8 tons of waste. And since the EPA calculates the cost of municipal waste disposal at about $100 per ton, the total cost to consumers of all waste disposal in the 10 years since 1990 is in excess of $1.1 trillion. It's hard to look at figures like that without starting to go a little cross-eyed.

The good news is that recycling has moved up on the political agenda. In the 1980s, fears that landfills were being overused and contaminated provided the motivation for increasing levels of recycling, and the highest producer of waste now has one of the best international records for recovery of waste. The last decade has seen an incredible drive to improve recycling levels. Of an estimated 269 million tons of waste in the United States in 1990, only 8 percent was recycled. By 1998, the amount of waste had increased to an estimated 340 million tons, but the recycled percentage had also increased—to an impressive 30 percent. More than 40 percent of all paper waste is recycled, as are nearly 30 percent of glass containers.

This revolution has been powered by the entrepreneurial spirit that exists in the United States. An efficient recycling system needs an end product for which there is a high demand; otherwise, the result is just another mountain of waste. Manufacturers in the United States found ways to make good use of recycled materials. Three-quarters of all the paper mills in the United States are set up to use recycled paper, which accounts for more than a third of the raw material used, according to the American Forest and Paper Association. The story is the same for plastic, except that here consumers can't keep up with the manufacturers; in 1995 *Business Week* reported that while the industry was demanding 800 million pounds of recovered plastic bottles, only 565 million pounds were actually collected.

By comparison, recycling in Britain stands, at present, at a much lower 9 percent, but the government has set a target of recovering 25 percent of household waste by 2005 and 30 percent by 2010. Although recycling garbage is the less glamorous end of organic living, it is extremely worthwhile in that it preserves precious resources, reduces consumption of fossil fuels, and so lowers the toxic load on the planet.

We can recycle three things: organic waste, water, and solid waste. Organic waste—vegetable peelings, old fruit, eggshells, and cold pasta, for example—should not be included in the garbage you put out on trash collection day. When organic waste is dumped in a landfill, it turns to methane, one of the greenhouse gases that causes global warming. Instead, if you have a garden, turn the organic waste into compost (see page 136 for instructions). Compost is a wonderful source of nutrients for the vegetable garden, and composting is part of nature's cycle—returning organic matter to the soil, which is where it came from. No organic household should be without a compost pile; if you don't have a garden, save your vegetable peelings for a friend who does.

Attitudes toward recycling have changed so much during the last 20 years that recycling paper is now routine in many countries.

recycling water

The way we use water is shamefully wasteful and uneconomic, but you can easily cut back in several ways: If you don't have a toilet that is designed to use less water, put a brick in the toilet tank; take showers rather than baths; put new washers on dripping faucets; and use your dishwasher or washing machine only for full loads. A washing machine can use up to 22 gallons of water per cycle, and two half-loads use more water than one full load.

If you have a flower garden or lawn, you could follow the example of Joseph Jenkins, author of the *Humanure Handbook*, which deals with numerous methods of recycling. Jenkins suggests draining "gray" water—soapy water from baths, showers, sinks, washing machines, and dishwashers—that would otherwise be sent down the drain to a sewage system for expensive purification. Instead, you can use this water in your yard to irrigate the land.

Despite the environmental benefits, this practice is illegal in parts of the United States because gray water may be contaminated with bacteria (although Jenkins suggests that the health risk is not significant). However, to minimize any risk, you should never store gray water and don't use it to water edible crops. The Center for Alternative Technology (CAT) also recommends reducing the amount of phosphates in the water by using environmentally friendly laundry detergents. Collecting water in a rain barrel is another way to reduce your water use in the garden during drier months. It's also better than chlorinated tap water for houseplants.

changing buying habits

According to the EPA, the average trash bin today is filled with paper (nearly 40 percent), glass (around 6 percent), plastics (about 9 percent) and metals, with a

Recycling the millions of plastic bottles that are thrown away each year is essential if we want to stop polluting the planet and wasting finite resources.

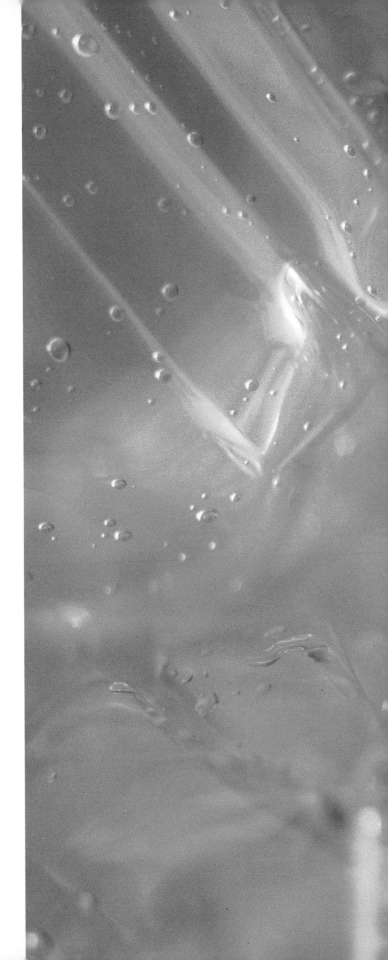

miscellany of dust, vegetable matter, and other materials on top of that. If we recycled those products we could begin to aim for a zero waste situation.

The very first step is to avoid buying anything that is not recyclable. The disposable diaper is a prime example of a product the public never knew it needed until it was invented. The EPA has calculated that the U.S. market alone generated about 3 million tons of disposable diapers in 1996. Given that the paper and plastics in the diapers take between 200 and 500 years to biodegrade, that is a huge quantity of long-lasting landfill. Disposable diapers also emit methane as they rot.

Organic cotton diapers produce less toxic waste during the manufacturing process and biodegrade more quickly than disposable diapers. They also eliminate the potential for health risks that come from the chemicals used in the manufacture of disposables—risks that have given some environmentalists cause for concern. Choosing nondisposable diapers may well be a case of better safe than sorry.

recycling household waste

The next step is to start recycling in your home. Why not begin with aluminum cans—recycling them saves 95 percent of the energy needed to create new cans from ore. Aim to recycle plastic, too—millions of plastic bottles are simply discarded worldwide every minute. Many plastic containers can be reused for food storage, and most recycling sites now accept plastic if you do have to throw items away. All paper and glass should be recycled: An abundance of recycling centers—and even curbside pickup in many areas—makes this easy. These may seem trivial steps, but when everybody takes them, the impact on our planet will be enormous.

People sometimes argue over whether it's more energy-efficient to recycle paper or burn it. The answer is certainly recycle: Recycling uses less energy and generates employment and income. Recycling cardboard cuts sulfur dioxide

emissions by half and saves about a quarter of the energy used in its manufacture. What's more, according to the Institute of Scrap Recycling Industries, the manufacturing process of recycled paper generates 74 percent less air pollution and 35 percent less water pollution and uses 50 percent less water and 64 percent less energy.

In both the United States and Britain, paper-recycling rates are high: The problem in Britain is that there is little demand for the end product. Britain needs to follow the U.S. example and create a good market for recycled products, so that it becomes a business, not just a voluntary chain.

The same is true for glass and plastics. The California clothing firm Patagonia seized on the technology that turns plastic soft-drink bottles into warm fleece garments and is now the market leader in this field. The point they're making is that mountain climbers and hikers who appreciate the environment need to help conserve it as well.

recycling incentives

The responsibility for building a successful recycling chain has to be divided among local authorities or states, consumers, and businesses. In Perkasie, Pennsylvania, the borough introduced an innovative pay-as-you-throw plan for garbage removal, providing a cost incentive to recycle. As a result, recycling rates rose to 46 percent in 1998. More communities need good collection systems so that people don't negate the benefits of recycling by driving their trash to the recycling center. Even better would be nationwide curbside collections.

Continuing to develop useful applications will keep demand for recyclables high. Thousands of products such as cereal boxes, nails, glass containers, and car bumpers now contain recycled materials. The most important point is that the cycle must be completed. But none of this can happen unless we separate our glass, paper, aluminum cans, and batteries, and stop tossing it all in the garbage can.

saving energy

The way we waste, or conserve, heat and light will have a huge impact on the planet we leave to our children. In the United States the production of electricity from fossil fuels causes more air pollution than any other source—including automobiles. Cutting down on the amount of power we use in our homes is one of the first steps to living organically. There is enormous scope for improving energy efficiency (the potential for savings in the United States is generally estimated at 30 to 50 percent). Finding sources of power that won't pollute the planet is better still.

A green architect once told me that most homeowners waste so much electricity through the poor design of their houses and their own bad habits that they might as well have huge holes punched through the walls of their living rooms. There are several ways of improving the way you and your home use power. Their cost-effectiveness can be measured in payback time: This is the amount of time it takes to earn back the initial financial investment in cost savings. Simple jobs that you can do yourself include insulating the attic—did you know that a quarter of your heat goes out through the

New technologies let you make highly efficient use of that most traditional form of heating, the wood-burning stove.

roof? Payback time on this, as on similar measures such as putting weather stripping around windows and doors, remembering to turn lights off, and taking showers instead of baths, is virtually nil. According to research, if you install attic insulation to a depth of 8 inches, you'll cut your heating costs by up to 20 percent.

Fiberglass made from recycled materials or, better still, polystyrene balls made from recycled packaging material make excellent insulation. Polystyrene isn't irritating to the user, is very lightweight for attic insulation, and never needs replacing. Plus, it means those packaging peanuts are recycled rather than sent to a landfill. Other environmentally friendly insulation materials include coconut fiber and flax. Avoid using pumped foam cavity insulation, which can be a source of fumes that may lead to sick building syndrome, even at home (see pages 124 to 127).

The most efficient insulation is a combination of wooden shutters at all the windows and heavy curtains to keep out drafts. These are more cost-effective than double or triple glazing, which reduces noise but has a long payback period. Other negative side effects of double glazing include raised humidity, an increased dust mite population, and increased concentrations of allergens and pollutants that may lead to a higher risk of allergies, hay fever, and asthma.

Of course, it's also important not to turn your home into a hermetically sealed box. The World Health Organization (WHO) recommends a complete air change every 2 hours. In a typical older house with sash windows and ill-fitting doors, the total volume of air is exchanged 16 times in 24 hours. A

left and above: *Green architects use innovative materials such as recycled glass blocks and skylights to flood the organic home with natural light and to save energy.*

modern house with triple glazing, weather stripping, roof insulation, and every conceivable energy-saving building extra only exchanges its air volume 2½ times in 24 hours—⅕ of the recommended WHO rate. So there is a compromise between a healthy atmosphere in which to live and raise your children and an over-obsession with energy conservation. A healthy home needs a few drafts.

Save energy and be healthier by turning down the thermostat on your central heating system, and improve air circulation by opening some windows. When you lower the temperature you'll have fewer dust mites, which in turn means fewer dust mite droppings: These are highly allergenic and the most common trigger of asthma and eczema.

It pays to keep an eye on new energy-efficient products, such as central heating boilers that recirculate flue gases and waste far less heat than the old-fashioned ones. Electric appliances in the home use an amazing amount of power. For example, a refrigerator made around 1990 uses more than 900 kilowatt hours per year—which is as much energy as you'd use if you left a 1,250 watt hairdryer on for a month. Ask the retailer or manufacturer about how efficiently the large domestic appliances use power, or look for the Energy Star logo, and buy accordingly. And don't forget all the smaller gadgets. Do you really need an electric carving knife? Or an electric egg beater or can opener?

green electricity

Among the many boom areas in green technology, the most exciting must be the arrival of green electricity. The last time we had a revolution in fuel, we came up with nuclear power. We seem to be doing a bit better this time: Wind power is the fastest growing energy resource in the world.

The production of electricity from fossil fuels accounts for huge percentages of global carbon dioxide and sulfur dioxide emissions, and large amounts of nitrogen oxide and mercury emissions, as well as fine airborne particles. Nuclear fuels produce high-level radioactive wastes, which will remain radioactive for between 10 and 25,000 years. All of these types of air pollution can result in a wide range of illnesses that cause thousands of deaths a year, as well as contributing directly to acid rain, global warming, and other environmental disasters.

The potential cost of these disasters is impossible to calculate, but the U.S. National Academy of Sciences has estimated that damage from acid rain adds up to about $6 billion annually, while damage from air pollution costs about $20 billion a year. The cost of global warming could be priceless.

If you're skeptical about the effects of global warming and aren't convinced by the recent meteorological disasters, consider the state of the Arctic in the year 2000. The Arctic ice pack has thinned from an average 10 feet in 1958 to 6 feet in the 1990s—a reduction of about 40 percent—and the extent of the ice cap is decreasing. Both of these trends are expected to continue. The evidence is undeniable: The Arctic ice cap is shrinking. The consequences for the global climate are enormous and will almost certainly include warmer temperatures (as less ice is available to reflect the sun's heat back into space) and more flooding.

In this context, all the excitement about the new electricity is entirely understandable. Wind power is flourishing globally. Germany has invested more than $2 billion in wind energy since 1990, and wind turbines are Denmark's leading export. In the United States, the Department of Energy (DOE) has promoted a program called Wind Powering America, which pledges to produce at least 5 percent of the nation's electricity from wind by 2020, with federal use of wind energy rising to 5 percent by 2010. In Britain, the pioneers who have installed efficient wind generators sell their surplus to the national grid. What could

Finding efficient ways to harness the enormous natural power of wind, water, and sun is a challenging but achievable task.

be better: electricity in your home, money in your pocket, and no polluting gases or chemicals.

How can we take part in this revolution ourselves? Four states (California, Pennsylvania, New Jersey, and Connecticut) in the United States have undergone a process of energy deregulation over the last 5 years. This means that consumers in those states can now choose from whom they buy their power. Buying green electricity is a concept that can be confusing, though. It doesn't mean that the power comes directly from a wind turbine, a solar collector, or one of the other renewable energy sources. But the electricity company will pledge to develop new green sources or buy green electricity themselves.

Green-e is one example of a renewable electricity program that helps consumers in the four states named above easily identify certified green electricity products and make responsible choices about the power they purchase. Consumers who choose electricity products with the Green-e logo can be sure that at least 50 percent of the electricity supply for the product comes from a renewable energy source such as water or wind. Over time, Green-e or similar programs will probably appear in other states as well.

solar and hydro power

If you really want to make a contribution to saving the planet, the ultimate energy source is solar power. Did you know that the sun delivers more energy to earth in 1 day than the total population of the planet could use in 27 years?

Domestic solar power comes in two forms: solar water heating and solar photovoltaics (PV). Solar water panels are increasingly affordable: You need only the panel and a tank in which to store the heated water, and payback time is estimated to be about 4 years for the cheapest varieties. You can even install the panels yourself. By contrast, PV panels,

The mighty power of the oceans is only one of the many renewable sources of energy that we are slowly learning to control.

which convert sunlight into electricity, are only for the very rich. There are net-metering schemes in some states in the United States that allow any excess power to be sold back to the grid, but it will still be a couple of decades before you make any money. However, costs are beginning to fall quickly, so it may not be long before we can all afford PV power.

Hydroelectricity—the production of energy through water power—is the most successful of all green energy sources, but it has caused huge debate. Up to 20 percent of the world's power is sourced from the massive dams that have been built in most countries over the last 70 years, but the environmental damage caused by their construction is immense: Valleys are flooded, homes are lost, and entire ecosystems may be wiped out. International pressure to re-think most dam-building projects is growing, and several U.S. dams are being dismantled as a result of grassroots pressure.

Harnessing the tidal flows in and out of estuaries has been proposed, but again, the environmental impact—in this case on wetland feeding grounds for waterfowl—makes it unlikely that any project will be viable in the foreseeable future. The force of an ocean wave is another source of natural power, but progress in taming this incredible energy is slow. A wave power device has recently begun generating electricity on the island of Islay in Scotland and is providing power for about 400 houses, but it may be a while before we, as consumers, feel the benefits on a large scale.

Using fast-running streams to power water wheels has little environmental impact: The wheels drive generators that produce enough power for immediate use and for battery charging. Other examples of energy production from renewable sources are relatively small-scale at present, although they have the potential to become extremely valuable. In North Carolina, the Blue Ridge RC&D Council is constructing a landfill gas-to-energy system that will be used to heat four greenhouses and a pottery business in nearby Burnsville. (The landfill was closed and capped in 1994.)

eco-style

If you want to live organically, you need to look at your entire style of living. A major part of this involves scrutinizing the contents of your home. Buy organic products—such as sheets, towels, and clothes made from organic cotton, and organic cleaning materials—as well as try to develop a "green" consciousness by considering how your way of life affects the planet.

The good news is that green living is fashionable. New developments and improvements in green design and understanding are cropping up every day—and that makes going green a positive pleasure.

clothing

Did you know that cotton crops account for just 3 percent of the world's farmland but are responsible for 15 percent of global pesticide use? Yet cotton can again become the pure

material it used to be if you choose organically grown cotton. Production of organic cotton has grown steadily in the United States since the 1980s, and demand is gradually increasing. Fashion designers like Giorgio Armani have been using undyed linen, organic cotton, and hemp in their collections, and the major retailers are following this lead.

Take a look inside your closet and find out what your clothes are made of. The best thing you can do for yourself and for the environment is to stay as natural as possible. Although man-made fibers were invaluable at the time of their invention, both polyester and nylon are manufactured from petrochemicals, which are nonrenewable and hugely polluting. They also use up a lot of resources during production and are not biodegradable. Polyvinyl chloride (PVC)—which is often used in the fashion industry to make raincoats—contains chlorine. Manufacturing PVC can result in the production of dioxin, as well as additives that have been linked to the development of asthma.

Viscose and rayon are both useful but are made from the pulp of fast-growing trees that require large amounts of water for growth and processing. The chemical treatments involved in their manufacture are not eco-friendly: Just four discharges of the acid used in the manufacture of viscose can alter the pH of an entire river.

The natural fiber hemp is one of the brightest hopes in the field of environmentally responsible materials. Its cultivation has been hampered by its relation to the cannabis plant (which is banned in the United States), but contrary to widespread beliefs, industrial hemp has no narcotic effect. It's a profitable crop that doesn't need insecticides or pesticides, making it environmentally friendly, especially for

left: *It is increasingly easy to buy attractive towels, bedding, and clothing made from unbleached or naturally dyed organic cotton.*
right: *Living an organic lifestyle need not mean sacrificing good design. Natural furnishing fabrics and painted floors are fashionable as well as eco-friendly.*

the farmers growing it. Hemp can be used for wonderful clothes fabric and canvas for shoes, turned into paper, and used to make animal feed, soaps, high-protein foods, and thousands of other products.

Another question to ask is how your clothes are produced. In the United States, organizations such as Sweatshop Watch are working hard to make consumers aware of the poor working conditions in which some of their clothes are made. If you want to play an active part in changing manufacturing practices in the garment industry worldwide, take a look at Sweatshop Watch's Web site at www.sweatshopwatch.org. The site provides information on how you can shop with a clear conscience as well as how you can help eliminate sweatshops in the garment industry.

In the meantime, remind yourself to look after your clothes properly and donate them to thrift shops or shelters when you no longer wear them.

furnishings

Asking about the source of the wood used to make your furniture is well worth it: The World Resources Institute reports that four-fifths of the planet's original forest cover has already been lost or degraded. Replanting takes place, but frequently the replanted forests are quick-grow cash crops, rather than the complex mixture of plants that creates the fragile ecosystem of our woods and rain forests. Take particular care to avoid mahogany, rosewood, ebony, and teak: These are all now endangered species.

But there is good news. Signs that big businesses are starting to take the issue of forest management seriously came in the summer of 2000, when Lowe's Companies, the world's second-largest home improvement retailer,

below and right: *Wooden flooring and natural floor coverings are better for your health than wall-to-wall carpets, which may have been treated with harmful chemicals.*

committed itself to purchasing green wood. All wood products carried in their stores will now come from well-managed, nonendangered forests, a policy prepared by the store with the help of activists at the Rainforest Action Network. You can find very good green furniture stores by looking on the Web. Check furniture to see whether the wood from which it is made has been stamped by the Forest Stewardship Council (FSC). This organization has a system in place that enables them to validate the origin of every piece of wood they've certified.

Carpets are another source of concern for environmentalists. Wall-to-wall carpeting is a source of dust mites and other allergens. In addition, most carpets are treated with synthetic dyes. They may also have been treated with chemicals to increase stain resistance and protect against moths, some of which may affect people with asthma or other respiratory problems. Check with the manufacturer if you are concerned about the chemicals used in a particular carpet because the carpet itself is unlikely to be labeled.

A healthy—and attractive—alternative to carpeting is to have natural wood, flagstone, or tile flooring, which is less allergenic and never needs replacing. Or, use natural floor coverings such as cork and coconut matting, natural rubber and linoleum, or hemp. Make sure these natural coverings have not been treated with chemicals during manufacture, and avoid all floorings made from synthetic materials. This includes vinyl, which is made from PVC.

buildings

Very few people have the chance to design their homes from start to finish. But if you do, it's worth getting hold of a green architect. The results can be spectacularly beautiful because green homes involve, by definition, the use of natural materials and good light. One architect told me he believed we have an emotional response to natural materials, like wood and stone, that we don't have to plastics and concrete— and I'm sure he's right.

When Greenpeace USA relocated its headquarters from U Street to Chinatown in Washington, D.C., only environmentally friendly materials were used in refurbishing the building. All the wood used was

(continued on page 123)

right and following pages: *Natural materials such as wood and stone make a house look warm and inviting.*

certified as sustainable by the Forest Stewardship Council; the carpet was made from recycled fibers and applied using a glue that doesn't emit toxic fumes; and the the bathroom tiles were made of recycled glass instead of vinyl, which is a common source of PVC pollution. In addition, photovoltaic solar panels on the roof generate electricity, while a solar thermal component produces hot water for the offices.

A straw house in London has provoked widespread admiration. The architect explains, "It works on passive energy principles with the heavily insulated straw-bale wall wrapping around the northeast and northwest elevations, while the south elevation is glass, to capture heat from the sun. The tower acts as a thermal flue, catching the wind and encouraging natural ventilation to cool the house in the summer." The result is comfortable and extremely attractive: Straw bales are no more flammable than synthetic building materials and allow a building to breathe.

The interaction of a building with its surroundings is at the heart of green architecture. The questions highest on the green architect's list are probably as follows: Can air pass in and out easily, providing good ventilation? Is energy used efficiently? Is there plenty of natural light? And obviously "will it look good?" is in there, too.

Using recycled materials is an important part of green building. There is a great network of people working in recycled and green building materials, and architectural salvage companies are an amazing source of every conceivable recycled building material. You can find old beams, reclaimed flooring, reused bricks, slates, tiles, iron-ware, girders, and plenty of things you never knew existed.

If you want something contemporary in style, use recycled glass blocks to make walls that are decorative and need no other treatment. They're available in clear, opaque, and even colored varieties, and they make wonderful shower screens, flooring, or partial room dividers. You can find these glass blocks in building centers and do-it-yourself stores.

Before you remove all the things that are considered "pollutants" in your home, it's important to understand that, although there has been some scientific research into these areas, the scientific community is often divided about the results. But there are some things we're sure about.

In 1989 the World Health Organization's International Agency for Research on Cancer declared the job of painting a high-risk carcinogenic occupation, with painters facing a 40 percent increased chance of contracting cancer. Putting a coat of paint on your windows or living with painted walls

left and above: *Wood is a surprisingly durable material that often looks better as it ages, making it ideal for recycling.*

Simple, traditional materials such as linen, cotten, and hemp are always attractive.

will not have the same effect, but we don't know enough about the cumulative effects of the chemicals in paints, wood finishes, varnishes, and all the other materials we have in our houses. Practitioners of environmental medicine believe that some solvents and other chemicals can be the cause of some of the increasingly common chronic and poorly defined illnesses like myalgic encephalomyelitis (ME)—sometimes derogatively called "yuppie flu"—and allergies. It's certainly worthwhile changing your decorative finishes if you or someone in your family suffers from this type of illness.

Painted walls are always popular, but you don't need to cover your walls in environmentally unfriendly paints when you can choose from a good selection of paints made with natural materials. The main ingredient in most natural paints is linseed oil, which works perfectly as a binder. It has been used in paintmaking for centuries, although the application today has various modern elements. Other ingredients include lime, chalk, and natural earth and mineral pigments. The resulting paint takes slightly longer to dry but smells far nicer, and by using natural paints you will be reducing the quantity of highly unpleasant waste washing out of the factory, as well as taking good care of your health.

Buying nontoxic paints is becoming easier by the week—even do-it-yourself stores now stock small supplies and specialty paint shops carry larger supplies of nontoxic milk paint and water-based paints, together with a range of more natural wood stains and finishes.

Many natural fabrics make excellent wall coverings: Linen, hemp, and cotton can all be used, and organic dyes are easily available if you want color rather than the natural effect. Industrial jute sacking is used widely in the horticultural industry and can be bought in rolls to make wall coverings that last a lifetime.

The tongue-and-groove boarding that is traditional in Scandinavia and parts of the United States makes a warm and permanent decorative finish. It needs no more than an occasional coat of beeswax or linseed oil and can last for centuries. In Britain, wood paneling is reserved mostly for grand houses and stately homes, except of course for beach houses, where wood panels are the traditional finish. Once again, if you're building a new home or doing a renovation project, check with your supplier to make sure that the wood comes from sustainable sources.

sick building syndrome

Our homes and offices are now filled with chemical treatments for every surface and corner: Construction Resources, a leading supplier of environmentally friendly building products in Britain, estimates that up to 90 percent of the internal surface area of a building may be covered with a synthetic petrochemical coat. The indoor environment—where we spend about 80 percent of our time—is probably even more polluted than the external environment.

Sick building syndrome (SBS) is a result of the combination of paints, varnishes, and other preparations that we breathe in constantly, and it is a well-documented problem. The EPA has produced an interesting fact sheet about SBS, which you can check out on its Web site. If you feel sick, breathless, and have headaches when you go to work, it may not be just because you don't like your boss.

A wide range of physical conditions are associated by some doctors and health practitioners with this cocktail of synthetic chemicals that we're breathing every day. The incidence of asthma has increased phenomenally in the last 20 years, simultaneously with the increase in use of pesticides and other chemical treatments. From 1980 to 1996, the number of Americans suffering from asthma more than doubled, and it's estimated that at least 5,000 Americans die from this respiratory disease every year. Along with asthma, different types of allergies have also increased exponentially. In Britain, allergies and chemical tolerance problems have doubled in the last 10 years.

Atmospheric pollution in your workplace could be worse than breathing in street-level fumes on a hot summer's day, according to one study. Our modern obsession with technology means that today's office is full of electrical equipment pumping ozone into the air we breathe for 8 hours or more each day. So what's wrong with that? Everyone is in a panic about the disappearing ozone layer in the atmosphere—and quite rightly—so surely ozone must be a good thing? Unfortunately, it's only good in the right place,

You can create a surprising range of textural effects with nontoxic paints, which are available in many colors.

and that's 20 or so miles above the earth, where it protects us from the sun's damaging ultraviolet rays. In your home, office, or out on the street, ozone is definitely bad news.

At street level, ozone is produced by a mixture of nitrogen oxides and other exhaust fumes interacting with oxygen on warm, sunny days. Gasoline, diesel, and industrial emissions all combine to create dreadful summer smog, laden with ozone, which irritates the healthiest of lungs and can have serious consequences for adults and children already suffering from asthma or other respiratory conditions. But in the workplace, whether that's home or office, an increase in unnoticeable ozone can also wreak such havoc. Eye, nose, and throat problems, recurrent headaches, dry skin and eczema, asthma, chronic fatigue, and never-ending colds and flu are evidence that all is not well at work.

Many factors contribute to sick office syndrome (SOS), a variant of SBS. New paint, carpets, and furniture, lots of dust-collecting open shelves and filing cabinets, too many workstations in large open-plan offices, poorly maintained air conditioning, inadequate office cleaning, volatile chemicals (such as marker pens, art materials, glues, solvents, and chemical cleaners), and little or no control of heating or ventilation all play their part. But the crucial unseen hazards are ozone and dry air: Each is bad enough on its own, but in combination they are a deadly duo.

Photocopiers, fax machines, computers, and laser printers—now basic equipment in every office—are the major producers of ozone pollution. And though the highly

toxic effects of ozone are well documented scientifically, few members of the general public are aware of the dangers. An open-plan office may have dozens of these machines working constantly, and you don't escape if you work from home. Converting the smallest bedroom into your office can mean even higher levels of ozone, and when both homes and modern office blocks have double glazing, draft exclusion, and central heating, the humidity can drop to levels normally found only in the Sahara Desert.

Dry air means dehydration of the protective mucous linings of the nose, sinuses, throat, and lungs, which increases the irritating effect of inhaled ozone. And research at the Center for Environmental Medicine and Lung Biology in the United States over the last 10 years has shown that exposure to ozone sensitizes the lining of the lungs in asthmatics, resulting in more severe attacks. Even in normally healthy lungs, ozone is a severe irritant and can sensitize lung tissue to other inhaled irritants, producing asthma-like episodes in nonasthmatics. The same is true for the mucous membranes lining the nose, throat, and sinuses: non–hay fever sufferers may experience prolonged symptoms of perennial rhinitis (constant mucous congestion, post-nasal drip, and repeated chest infections).

While the average outdoor humidity level will vary depending upon what climate you live in, the healthiest, most comfortable level in an indoor working environment should be a minimum of 50 percent. Most electronic offices fall significantly below this comfort zone, leading to dry, sore eyes (a serious hazard for contact-lens users), dry, sore throats, and dry, itchy skin. Feeling static shocks around the office is a certain indicator that humidity is much too low.

Professor Jonathan Brostoff, an allergy expert in London and president of the British Allergy Foundation, told me of

A single stem of Buddleia davidii, *the butterfly bush, looks striking in a simple vase.*

his concerns regarding ozone: "Ozone can be a potent, unseen irritant to the linings of the nose and lungs. If you are already allergic, these linings are irritated and inflamed, and ozone could make it much worse. Open a window if you can, and keep drinking lots of fluids to avoid dehydration."

Another serious lung irritant are the particulates—tiny particles of carbon—that are produced by fax machines, photocopiers, and printers. This dust is known to cause lung problems after prolonged exposure; in a confined space, even a few hours' exposure can be enough to have serious consequences (for example, an acute cough that develops into chronic bronchitis in susceptible individuals). Iron and silica, both present in toner dust, have been found in the lungs of affected workers. The irritant effect is magnified by the high ozone levels already mentioned, so good ventilation and higher humidity are essential to protect against it.

A small desktop humidifier or a combined ionizer and carbon filter will remove ozone and particles from a small office or home. Large commercial machines that humidify and clean the air are available for big office spaces.

Nature can provide us with remedies for some of the problems of SOS. Green, leafy plants remove toxic chemicals from the air, especially benzene, formaldehyde, and fumes from cleaning fluids. Spider plants and ivy work extremely well, also absorbing ozone. Central heating and electronic equipment such as computers, photocopiers, and printers all create dry, dusty atmospheres that can be improved greatly by the health-giving moisture vapor released into the air by leafy plants. Bamboos, palms, ferns, and ornamental fig plants are among the best plants for the job.

Finally, brighten up the workplace with flowers. Stress, anxiety, and mental fatigue are all improved by the sight of a growing plant or a simple bunch of flowers.

Fill your home and workplace with as many green leafy plants as possible to help absorb toxic chemicals from the air.

7 STEPS TO A HEALTHY OFFICE

1. Switch off all electrical equipment when not in use—don't leave it in standby mode.

2. In winter, place humidifiers on or near heaters—in desperation, a wet towel will do.

3. In summer, open windows if you have them, and ask employers to install humidifiers.

4. Drink at least 1½ quarts of water (other beverages don't count) during the working day.

5. Create a microclimate around your workspace with green plants or a desktop humidifier or air cleaner.

6. In winter, turn central heating thermostats down by about 5 degrees, and in summer turn air conditioning up by 5 degrees to save energy and reduce dehydration.

7. Don't eat lunch at your desk. Instead, get out in the fresh air, even if it's raining.

eco-friendly household products

The fact that we allow household cleaners to affect the environment as they do is frustrating, but we can take heart in knowing that it's relatively easy to take preventive action and that environmentally friendly companies are beginning to gain international reputations.

In fact, the effects of household cleaners brought environmental issues into the political spotlight when scientists in the United States discovered that Lake Erie, one of the five Great Lakes, was dying because of phosphate poisoning. During the 1950s, laundry detergent manufacturers realized that adding phosphate to their product would make clothes look whiter than white. Phosphate acts as a fertilizer (just like nitrogen, which has a similar effect in salt water) and, when released into lakes, rivers, or ponds, makes the algae grow faster and for longer periods of time. The result is that other species in the water are deprived of light and oxygen, and the water "dies." Although laundry detergent isn't the only source of phosphate (human excrement is one of the richest sources, for example), the new powders meant there was a lot more phosphate to end up in rivers and streams.

The specter of Lake Erie's death forced the governments of both the United States and Canada, who border the lake, to cooperate. The governments banned phosphate-containing detergents in the area and in many places across both countries.

Other pollutants in household cleaners include hydrocarbons, which contribute to the greenhouse effect; chlorine, found in some bleaches; and formaldehyde, used in some room deodorizers and air fresheners. Formaldehyde is listed as hazardous by the United States Agency for Toxic Substances and Disease registry.

Household cleaners can also have a negative impact on your health. The EPA warns about the effect of volatile organic compounds (VOCs), such as carbon tetrachloride (a cleaning agent) and toluene, a widely used industrial solvent, that are common causes of dermatitis: "The ability of VOCs to cause health effects varies greatly, from those that are highly toxic, to those with no known health effect. As with other pollutants, the extent and nature of the health effect will depend on many factors, including level of exposure and length of time exposed. Eye and respiratory tract irritation, headaches, dizziness, visual disorders, and memory impairment are among the immediate symptoms that some people have experienced soon after exposure to some VOCs. At present, not much is known about what health effects occur from the levels of VOCs usually found in homes. Many organic compounds are known to cause cancer in animals; some are suspected of causing, or are known to cause, cancer in humans."

Some air fresheners and fabric sprays reputedly work by blocking your sense of smell and attacking the tiny hairs in your nasal passages. So try to avoid them all, and rely on natural smells such as dried herbs or genuine aromatherapy fragrancers, which smell more pleasant than artificial room fresheners and contain none of the highly irritant chemicals to which many people are sensitive.

Huge numbers of people have found that aromatherapy massage helps many physical and emotional problems. Home-based aromatherapy is great for minor ailments, and using an essential oil fragrance helps insomnia, headaches, sinus problems, coughs, colds, stress, anxiety, and a host of other problems. The same is not always true with so-called aromatherapy candles. Most contain little, if any, real essential oils but are perfumed with more of the synthetic chemical fragrances. Lots of people, particularly those with asthma, react badly to them, so use these candles only if they contain real oils.

An increasingly wide selection of environmentally friendly household products is available at very competitive prices. Although it's impossible to manufacture cleaners

A salt-water solution is a simple and effective cleaner that is much safer than the cocktail of chemicals found in most cleaning cabinets.

without any environmental impact at all, you can use household cleaners that are less harmful to the environment. So choose products that don't contain phosphates and are 100 percent biodegradable.

Best of all, why not get under your sink and throw away those bottles full of chemicals? What do you need them for? (Call your local municipality or trash collection service to find out how to dispose of chemical products like insecticides, stain removers, and bleaches safely.) Try some of the old-fashioned cleaners—they work just as well, and you don't have to worry about your children getting hold of them.

Baking soda, for example, can serve as a scouring powder, a polish, and a cleaner. Or shake it onto the carpet before vacuuming, and you'll pick up more dust. You can even use it as a fungicide. Instead of using the contents of all those purchased plastic bottles, try cleaning with vinegar, lemon juice, citrus oil, an onion, or just plain salt water. Soak brass candlesticks in bean cooking water, and they will shine brilliantly. Eucalyptus oil can take grease stains out of any material without leaving a mark, ink stains can be lifted with lemon juice, and calcium deposits on irons or showerheads can be removed with a strong vinegar solution. And elbow grease is free. Remember, there are plenty of quick and cheap ways to get things clean without having to resort to the heavy guys.

... the organic garden

The kiss of the sun for pardon,
The song of the birds for mirth,
One is nearer God's heart in a garden
Than anywhere else on earth.

Dorothy Frances Gurney (1858–1932)

A garden can offer some of the most uncomplicated happiness known to man or woman. If you love gardening and love your garden, then you must think seriously about making it organic. An organic garden is healthier for the soil, for the plants growing in it, and for you—and it's one more contribution to the survival of our planet. It can also be a starting point for introducing children to the joys of gardening and the pleasures of eating fresh, chemical-free produce.

Giving your children a corner of the garden as their own to grow simple things like radishes, lettuce, carrots, and beans will encourage them to eat what they grow. Getting youngsters on the right nutritional path at an early age establishes healthy eating patterns that will stay with them for life. Only if your garden is organic can you in good

Adding plenty of organic matter such as homemade compost creates dark, fertile soil that is the key to success in an organic garden.

conscience allow your children to get their hands in the soil and eat the produce they grow.

People outline different fundamental principles for organic gardening, but the soil is always the starting point. Healthy soil, plenty of compost, and choosing plants that are right for your growing conditions and that have shown good resistance to pests and diseases are three key ingredients of organic gardening. If you have all three, you're already on the right path.

Once you have all the fundamentals, a few other techniques will help your garden flourish without chemicals. Inviting good bugs into your garden to eat pest insects, for instance, helps control bad bugs without using harmful insecticides. And mulching between plants helps keep weeds at bay (and helps conserve soil moisture) so that you don't have to reach for the bottle of herbicide.

You might think that gardening organically is more difficult than gardening with chemicals—but it's not. And it actually saves you money because you don't have to buy pesticides and herbicides or spend time applying them.

So read on to find out just how you can garden organically. Before you know it you'll be eating your very own pesticide-free potatoes or tomatoes, grown just a step from your kitchen window, or cutting your own organically grown flowers for a beautiful bouquet.

planning your garden

This is the moment when you sit down, grab pen and paper, and think about what you want to do with the space in front of you. What is your ideal garden? Would you like a quiet space filled with flowers and sweet smells, or do you want a hard-working kitchen garden where you can harvest wonderful lettuces and tomatoes every day for the freshest salads you can imagine? Or are you hoping for a combination of the two: decorative and functional at the same time? Personally, I think vegetables can be as ornamental as rose bushes or rhododendrons. Why not grow globe artichokes at the back of your flower bed or shrub border, runner beans amid the dahlias, or garlic around the roses, where it will help keep pests like aphids at bay?

When thinking about what you want to grow, also consider the conditions of your yard. Do you have lots of sun, lots of shade, or a little of both? Do you have areas with good drainage, and others where water pools after a rain? These are important questions to consider, as one of the keys to successful organic gardening is growing plants in the conditions they like best. Some plants thrive in full sun, while others need full or partial shade. The same goes for moisture—some plants like to have wet feet, and others like their soil on the dry side.

If you have enough room, leave part of the garden a little wild—or plant a small wildflower garden—to create a habitat for butterflies and other beneficial insects. If you decide on wildflowers, don't be fooled by the colorful seed packets that promise an instant wild meadow—they don't

work. Your lawn grass will compete with the seed and choke out the plants before they get established. Instead, plant the seeds in pots in fall and allow them to grow in a greenhouse; then harden them off outside during the summer and plant them in individual clumps on your cleared soil in the fall.

learning about your soil

The first step in organic gardening involves finding out what type of soil you have: clay, sand, or silt. Knowing your soil type is important because it will help you choose plants that are most likely to grow easily in the type of soil you have. You can also amend the soil to give your preferred plants optimum growing conditions.

If you're not sure what kind of soil you have in your garden, grab half a handful, dampen it, and try to roll it into a sausage. Soil that doesn't hold together is probably sandy. A soil sausage that breaks when you try to bend it is silt; if you can form a ring out of the sausage you have clay soil.

Clay is the heaviest of all the soil types and is very fertile and nutrient rich. But it can also be rock-hard in summer and a muddy mess the rest of the time. The trick with clay is to improve the soil structure by digging as much organic material as possible into the surface soil—the more the better. Digging in coarse sand will also improve drainage, but you have to add a lot of sand for it to be effective. (And sand won't improve the nutrient levels of your soil.) After a couple of years of amending your soil, you should see a marked improvement. Just remember never to tread on your soil when it's wet or you'll pack it all together again. (This goes for all soil types; if you need to work on a wet bed, put a plank across the soil and walk on that.)

Sandy soil is at the opposite extreme: light and easy to work, but incapable of holding water well and lacking most nutrients. Again, you can easily improve it by working in organic matter, which will improve its water- and nutrient-retention capacity. Mulching also helps retain moisture.

Silt soils are like clay in many ways: They pack down easily and drain badly. But as with clay, generous helpings of organic matter dug in will eventually improve things.

When it comes to adding organic matter to the soil, many gardeners reach for peat moss, which helps improve moisture retention and drainage. However, centuries-old peat bogs are being destroyed for the gardener's convenience, and with them the habitat of flora and fauna that thrive in those conditions. Good alternatives to peat include well-composted organic animal manure or, best of all, your own homemade compost.

Test your soil to find out its pH level: Depending on whether it's alkaline (high pH) or acid (low pH), different plants will be able to thrive in it. You can buy a simple test kit at your local garden center. If you need to make an acidic soil more alkaline, you can add lime, which will have a gradual effect over time—but why fight nature? Take a look around your neighborhood and see which gardens you like best. Most likely they'll be full of plants that suit the local soil and climate conditions, so borrow some ideas from them.

Having your soil tested to find out its nutrient levels is also a good idea. The test kits available at garden centers usually aren't accurate enough to be helpful, so you'll need to send a soil sample to a testing lab. Call your local Cooperative Extension Service for details. The results will be invaluable when it comes to fertilizing your soil.

suiting the garden to your site

Once you know what kind of soil you have, the next step is to look at all the other physical aspects of your garden.

★ Is it full of sun or deep in shade?

★ Is the site windy or is it a sheltered spot?

★ Are there patches of poorly drained soggy ground?

★ Are there trees that you want to keep?

★ Are there boulders that you might want to move?

★ Are there slopes that might need terracing?

Take all these factors into consideration when you decide what plants to grow and where you want to put any new structures, but you don't have to level the site or clear it of every tree stump, rock, wet area, or clump of shady trees. Each of these features can be used to your advantage to make special insect and animal habitats as well as provide enormous interest in your garden. If you have a boggy area, turn it into a wetland garden. Then you can grow plants that prefer to have wet feet, like hostas, flag irises, and cattails (*Typha* spp.). Rocks and boulders can be the basis for a fern garden, and shady areas are wonderful homes for woodland plants and for naturalizing snowdrops (*Galanthus* spp.), bluebells (*Hyacinthoides* spp.), hyacinths, and daffodils.

building the framework

It makes good sense to sort out all the structural details—like making paths and patios or building walls, fences, garden sheds, and barbecue areas—before you start planting. You will also need to find suitable spots for solar-powered lighting, water pumps and fountains, or other permanent fixtures before you plant your vegetable patch or flower bed. Your local nursery or garden center can advise you about the most suitable methods and materials to use for your needs, or you can find the information in any good organic gardening book. Just make sure that any wood you use isn't treated with chemical wood preservatives and that it's harvested from green sustainable sources. Use quarried or naturally collected stone for paths and patios rather than soft sandstone or limestone. In some areas their removal is destroying important natural habitats.

(continued on page 136)

following pages: *A shed is the gardener's traditional refuge from the elements and, provided it's well ventilated and frost free, it also makes a good place to dry strings of onions and garlic, to ripen tomatoes at the end of the growing season, and to pot up plants and bulbs.*

There is no doubt that a greenhouse can be a useful addition to the organic garden if you want to grow seedlings or tender plants and fruits that need reliable warmth and shelter. But for many gardeners both space and time are at a premium, and a greenhouse certainly demands both. On the other hand, a shed takes up space, but you will probably find one useful for storing your tools safely.

If you do have a shed, greenhouse, or other building in the garden, install rain barrels to collect runoff water for watering your plants. You can also connect barrels to your house downspouts. Using recycled water in the garden helps conserve this precious resource.

siting your compost heap

Methods of making compost are described on the opposite page, but when planning your garden you need to decide where to locate the heap (or heaps—two piles or even three are ideal because you can turn the piles from one bin to the other). Choose a spot that's not too far from either your kitchen or the vegetable garden, if possible, so that unloading compost buckets will be less of a chore. The site should not be cold or shaded. The ideal size heap for the hot composting method that I recommend is 3 square feet; if your heap is smaller than this, it won't heat up properly.

There are numerous types of ready-made containers on the market, but it is really very easy to build your own. All you need is four recycled wood pallets. Nail them together to form a box and cover the structure with chicken wire, for a good bin at very modest cost. For easier access to the compost, use just three pallets in a U shape, leaving the front of the bin open so you can easily turn or use your compost. If you are feeling extravagant, you can invest in a compost bin that can be rotated so you won't have to turn your compost manually.

caring for your garden

When it comes to organic gardening, paying attention to what's going on in your garden is one of the easiest ways to give it good care. If you stroll through your garden regularly, you'll notice any potential problem and be able to take care of it before it has a chance to get out of hand.

THE BENEFITS OF RAISED BEDS

When you are planning your garden, consider building raised beds for your vegetables: They'll give you deep beds of good soil, and you can plant everything closer together. This means your vegetables will take up less space and weeds won't have much room to take hold. You'll also be less likely to walk on the bed and compact the soil. If they are built sufficiently high, raised beds are great for disabled gardeners or anyone with back problems, as they reduce the need for a lot of bending.

I recently created a raised-bed organic herb garden. Because my soil is very heavy clay, I've had problems growing root vegetables that need deep, loose soil. Now I can plant carrots, parsnips, and horseradish in the raised beds with the herbs.

Frame your raised beds in wood, brick, or stone, depending on your budget and preferences. Whatever type of frame you use, the success of your beds depends on what goes inside. If you're making raised beds over turfgrass, put down several layers of dampened newspaper and then add 6 to 8 inches of garden topsoil mixed with compost. If your bed is being built over an existing garden, adding 3 to 4 inches of soil should be plenty. If the soil is too heavy, add some sand to the mix.

fertilizing

The most important task for an organic gardener is feeding the soil with large amounts of organic matter, such as homemade compost. This in turn feeds the plants with the nitrogen (N), phosphorus (P), and potassium (or potash; K) as well as micronutrients that are all essential for healthy growth. Applying large quantities of organic matter will also improve the structure of your soil, particularly if it is clay or sand, making it easier for your plants to get the nutrients they need from the soil.

The synthetic chemical fertilizers used by conventional gardeners often give plants an unnaturally high boost of nitrogen, encouraging them to grow lots of leaves and fewer flowers or fruits. If you're feeding your soil with plenty of organic compost and keeping it covered with organic mulch, then your plants really should be getting all the nutrients they need. However, if your garden is new or you're growing heavy feeders such as broccoli and tomatoes, you can give them a boost.

Liquid fertilizers such as seaweed extract, fish emulsion, and compost tea are good for booster feedings because their nutrients are quickly available to plants. They're particularly suitable and convenient to use for container plants. Dry organic fertilizers include bloodmeal, bonemeal, alfalfa meal, and rock phosphate. Apply these by side-dressing, or working them into the top 1 inch of soil around the plants. Make sure these fertilizers don't actually touch the plants. The benefit of these fertilizers is that they provide a slow release of nutrients to your plants, rather than a quick burst.

Leafmold is invaluable and it's easy to make, although it may take a year or more until it's ready to use. Simply gather fallen leaves and pile them together in a wire container or in a large sack and let them decompose. They're broken down by fungus, so keep them moist. The resulting material can be used as a mulch to deter weeds or worked into the top layer of the soil to improve its structure and nutrient content.

making compost

Organic gardeners are very enthusiastic about their compost, which is simply decomposed organic matter (including fruit and vegetable wastes, coffee grounds, and crushed eggshells from your kitchen; grass cuttings; fallen leaves; and perhaps some old straw and faded flowers). All these plant-based materials go in one heap to sit and rot, and in the end they produce perfect compost. Good compost has been described as "brown and crumbly with the sweetest of smells, like woods in autumn."

The most effective compost heaps are built up all at once and left to decompose. This method is known as hot composting, since the pile reaches a high temperature while decomposing, which speeds the process (the compost may be ready in as little as 2 months) and helps to kill weed seeds. Keep your compost material stacked beside the bin until you are ready to start. You can add to your compost pile from time to time or even daily, but it will take longer to turn into finished compost. To speed things up, shred any woody material before composting. Otherwise it will take too long to decompose.

Don't put diseased plant material onto your compost heap (especially anything with obvious mildew or fungus infections) because the diseases will permeate the pile. Discard them and all perennial weeds with your trash. Also do not include any meat or dairy foods scraps, as these can attract unwanted scavangers to your compost pile.

Start your compost pile so it's about 3 feet square and 3 feet high, or build up the layers in a bin. Put about 1 foot of twiggy material at the bottom to let air into the heap (good air circulation is a crucial part of composting, so you will also need to stir or turn the pile occasionally), and then cover that with about 6 inches of the waste material. Add the compost ingredients in layers, starting with wet green waste, such as grass cuttings, cut flowers, or fruit and vegetable peelings. Alternate with dry brown waste, such as dead leaves.

AMAZING EARTHWORMS

The humble earthworm will have statues built to him (or her) one day. Charles Darwin thought they were fantastic, and said, "It may be doubted whether there are many other animals which have played so important a role in the history of the world as these lowly organized creatures." Why all this enthusiasm? Because earthworms chomp their way through the organic matter of our soil, breaking it up as they go, so that roots, air, and water can come through. Without worms, plants can suffer.

Earthworms have been around for a few millennia, and there are over 3,000 species. Some types will be happy in your compost heap, while others thrive in the soil. These blind creatures have plenty of natural predators. Both birds and moles love nothing better than a good worm dinner, and robins can actually hear worms moving underground—that's why robins cock their heads to the side. Worms are so precious that it really is worth buying them if they are scarce in your garden. They are not lookers, but we shouldn't judge by appearances.

If you want to make perfect compost for growing seedlings, then worms are your best friends. Every organic garden should have a worm compost bin; if your garden is small, you can even keep the worm bin in the kitchen. Commercial versions are readily available from all good garden suppliers. They usually comprise an interlocking combination of a collecting tray, working trays, a drainage spout, and a lid. You'll also need to buy worms— they're usually sold separately. Redworms are the most common type of worms used for this purpose.

Put the worms at the bottom, and the kitchen vegetable waste into the tray above. The worms eat their way through layer after layer. When the bottom layer is finished, empty it and put that container on the top and start to fill it with kitchen waste. Stale bread, uneaten pasta, vegetable peelings, banana skins—all can be added little by little to your worm compost bin. The end product is very rich and makes a perfect potting or growing medium when mixed with fine organic bark and sand.

To get your compost started quickly, you can sprinkle in a compost activator that you can buy in most gardening centers. But adding some garden soil or spent compost will work just as well. Keep building up the layers until you reach the top, making sure the material you add is moist, and finish with a brown layer. Then cover the bin or pile and leave it to get working.

The temperature of the heap will rise as it decomposes; when the center of the pile doesn't seem quite as hot, turn the heap over and let the temperature rise again. The compost is ready when the heap is cool and the mix is rich, brown, and crumbly.

Green garden or kitchen waste is full of nutrients that can be returned to the soil in the form of compost.

preparing the garden bed

To dig or not to dig: An increasing number of organic experts believe that digging should be avoided after the initial preparation of a bed, since turning soil over can damage its structure and kill important and valuable bacteria by exposing them to the elements. No-dig techniques include applying layers of organic material (such as leaves, newspaper, shredded bark, and grass clippings) on a regular basis. They are slowly incorporated into the soil through the activity of rain, frost, and worms rather than by digging.

Traditional nondiggers work with raised beds or divide their vegetable plot into smaller beds with paths in between. The beds should be narrow enough to work from either side so you don't ever have to stand on them (which will compact the soil). Some organic gardeners lay old newspapers between the beds to make a better working surface. Newspaper can also be used as a mulch through which to plant strawberries, as well as potatoes and other root crops. The paper not only conserves moisture but prevents excessive weed growth.

Of course, there's nothing wrong with digging a new garden bed. It's just more labor intensive. You'll have to clear the spot where you want your garden to be. For instance, if your garden area is covered in turfgrass, you'll need to cut the turf out with a spade. Slice under the turf with your spade and lift it in thin slabs. Pile the cut turf, grass side down, a foot or two high. Keep the pile moist, and the next year it will be a great soil amendment to add to your garden.

Once the grass is removed, you're ready to cultivate the soil and get it ready for planting. Hand tilling is much better for the soil than using a rotary tiller to work the soil. Digging by hand lets you carefully remove roots, runners, and other parts of perennial weeds as you work. A powerful rotary tiller can chop up those roots and runners into smaller pieces, which may then resprout into new weeds.

After tilling the soil, spread a 1-inch layer of compost over the surface of the soil with a garden rake. Then use a shovel or digging fork to dig it in by hand. A fork will be your best bet if your soil is rocky or if you're removing those roots and runners.

As you dig, work from one end of the bed to the other, turning the soil over to the depth of your shovel or fork. Break up large clumps of soil with your tool and remove rocks and weeds as you go. Be sure not to stand on the soil that you just turned or you'll compact all the loose, fluffy texture you've just worked so hard to create.

planting seeds

When you're ready to plant seeds, refer to the seed packets for information about when to sow and how deep to plant.

Be sure to look at the date on the seed packets before you buy them. Old, stale seed won't germinate reliably, so be sure to buy only seeds marked for the current growing season.

Some plants don't adapt all that well to transplanting, and they are best started directly in the garden from seed. If you intend to include beans, beets, carrots, cucumbers, peas, potatoes, salad greens, squash, or sweet corn in your vegetable garden, I suggest starting them outdoors from seed.

To plant your seeds, draw a slightly deeper furrow than recommended on the seed packet, fill the furrow halfway with a mixture of fine compost and soil, then sow your seeds. You can cover the seeds with more of the compost mixture, or you can rake in the edges of the furrow if your soil is in good condition. Simply water well and wait for the seedlings.

starting with transplants

It is possible to grow almost all plants from seed, though some are more difficult than others. There are specialty seed catalogs that market organic seeds, but I would strongly advise a beginning gardener to buy organic plants to start with. You can always save seed from your vegetables or flowers to plant for the next season.

Whether you're planting vegetables or flowers, transplants will give your garden an instant start. When you visit the garden center to buy your transplants, be sure to look for seedlings that have short, thick, sturdy stems and deep green foliage. Avoid plants with yellowed, curled, mottled, or misshapen leaves. Also be wary of plants that are too big for their containers. They probably won't have a very good root structure. In fact, lift the plant out of its container to check the roots and make sure they aren't potbound. White tips indicate healthy, growing roots.

It's also a good idea to check out the underside of the leaves to look for insect eggs or pests such as aphids,

A thick mulch of bark chippings is a particularly effective and attractive form of weed control in ornamental flowerbeds.

whiteflies, and spider mites. There's no sense in bringing home unwanted garden visitors!

Just as some vegetables grow best when they're directly sown outdoors in the garden soil, you'll be better off planting others as transplants. Crops that like cool weather, like broccoli and cabbage, would take too long to mature in some climates if they're started as seed, so buy transplants and enjoy the harvest. Other vegetables that can't be planted outside until the soil is nice and warm, such as tomatoes and peppers, would get such a late start that planting transplants ensures that you'll be able to harvest them much sooner than if you had started with seeds.

You can move transplants right into your prepared garden bed as soon as you get them home. For best results, choose an overcast day, or plant later in the afternoon so the sun and wind exposure won't harm them before they can settle in.

Use a trowel to dig a hole that's fairly deep and about 1½ times as wide as the container. Tap the plant out of the container and put it in the hole you've prepared. Fill the hole around the rootball and pat the soil firmly so it's level around the plant. Water each transplant as soon as you've planted it. That's it. Of course, if it's very sunny, you may want to give your transplants a bit of shade. A propped-up piece of cardboard works well. If the weather is still cool, protect your transplants by putting paper bags over them at night. (You can weigh their edges down with small rocks.)

weeding and mulching

Weeding can prove to be a test of your hoeing and picking skills. But organic gardeners have a great weapon to use in the weed war—mulching. Sooner or later, any discussion about organic gardening seems to get around to this topic.

To an organic gardener, mulching means covering the soil surface with a thick layer of organic materials such as shredded bark, shredded leaves, or grass clippings—not black plastic. Any of these block out the light, which in turn

kills off annual weeds. In addition, because they're organic, these mulch materials rot into the soil, adding more nutrients. They also help your soil retain moisture by preventing surface evaporation. Mulching works well for all types of soil, particularly sandy soil.

Of course, the downside to using an organic mulch such as compost or grass cuttings is that tenacious weeds can make their way through it. If you are going to use a mulch of organic materials, make sure the soil is already weeded, and that the layer you put down is thick enough to stop any more from coming through. One way to prevent weeds from growing through mulch is to add a few layers of damp newspaper beneath your preferred mulch. It will eventually decompose (it's a favorite of earthworms!), but until that happens, it provides a good barrier to weeds. Simply cover it with a more attractive organic mulch.

Well-composted manure, compost, and leafmold are the most nutritious mulches, but save the composted manure to use on ornamental plants—it's not for edibles. There are many other options to choose from, such as pine or spruce needles or the traditional straw for strawberries—it repels slugs and is said to improve the flavor. My personal preference is wood chips, which look and smell attractive.

fighting pests and diseases

Organic gardeners are as strongly opposed to pesticide use as organic farmers are, and with good reason. It is appalling that statistically gardens have more chemicals poured on to them per square yard than big-business farms. This cannot be good for our health or for the health of the planet.

As an organic gardener, you can use a range of weapons to fight off pests and diseases—including patience and your imagination. Vigilance is necessary—it's a lot easier to stop an infestation if you spot bugs early. You must be prepared to pick grubs out of the soil by hand or turn over every cabbage leaf to catch those hungry

caterpillars. In the end, it will be much healthier for you and your plants than spraying them with pesticides. Besides, not all insects are bad.

One way to prevent pest or disease problems from taking hold in the first place is to choose species that are resistant to pests and diseases. Plant a wide variety of plants and your garden will attract friendly predator insects, too. If they're not effective at eating all the pests, then you can try biological control, which involves buying a parasite to feed on the relevant pest. For example, a lot of work has been done on microbial insecticides—which use very specific insect diseases to kill them off. The best known is *Bacillus*

thuringiensis (BT). BT prevents caterpillars from eating, thereby killing them. Varieties of pests that are resistant to BT have recently developed as a result of its use in genetically modified crops, but it can still be effective in a home garden.

You can also try physical barriers such as fabric row covers to prevent pests from reaching your plants. (Just be sure to uncover them when they flower so the pollinators can do their job, or you won't have any vegetables to harvest.) Plastic rings cut from soft-drink bottles and set around seedlings will protect them from cutworms. Traps can be

Picking caterpillars and beetles off your vegetables before they have a chance to do harm is an effective form of organic pest control.

extremely effective, too. Sticky traps attract whiteflies off tomatoes and keep aphids away from cabbages, broccoli, brussels sprouts, peas, and beans. Hanging colored sticky traps in fruit trees will trap fruit flies, while beer traps will help keep down the slug population (sink a shallow dish into the ground, fill it with beer, and wait for the slugs to fall in).

Spray-type controls should be the last resort. There are certain pesticides that are organic, such as insecticidal soaps,

although they can also kill beneficial insects as well as pests. The best solution is to grow strong, healthy plants. Pests much prefer the weak, sappy specimens that often grow in overfertilized conventional gardens.

Diseases can be controlled by choosing disease-resistant varieties, but the healthier your plants, the less problem you'll have. There will still be an occasional disheartening moment when you have to pull out a beloved shrub or perennial because disease has set into the soil, but you'll soon discover which plants work best in your yard and which ones are best left at the garden center.

Alliums (above left) *and marigolds are both used as companion plants; choose French marigolds (*Tagetes patula) *rather than the less effective pot marigold (*Calendula officinalis) (right).

COMPANION PLANTING

Discouraging pests by means of companion planting is an idea that divides organic farmers: Some like it; others report low success rates. The idea is to grow beneficial plants next to ones that are susceptible to pests.

For example, when members of the onion family (*Allium* spp.) are planted near roses, they're said to repel aphids (and chives actually make a beautiful border for roses). Basil reputedly helps tomatoes to resist insects and disease, such as whiteflies and mildew. Beautiful, colorful nasturtiums are supposed to deter blackflies and whiteflies, but the most successful result I have had is with French marigolds, which really do attract hoverflies. When the hoverflies are in the neighborhood, aphid populations decline rapidly. Feverfew is thought to be an insect repellent, as is mint. (Mint also repels mice and rats, and if you have some in the house, it may keep moths away).

This is an area where you may have to experiment for yourself. Besides, it's great fun—and deeply satisfying if you get good results.

choosing plants

If you are like me, some of the happiest moments in planning your garden will be spent looking through seed catalogs and choosing plants. Let your imagination run wild for a while, mark all the 500 different varieties you want, then calm down and pare down your list. It's easy to get carried away, but you really need to consider whether your garden has the right conditions to grow the plants that you have set your heart on. Here's one tip: If you're starting from scratch, decide what you want and get going. But if you inherited a garden planted by a previous owner, it's worth waiting a year to see what is in the beds.

If you are new to the area, try and find out what particular pests and diseases crop up around you. If you are replanting your old garden, think back to the problems you have faced in the past. Once you have listed the problems, try to find varieties of plants that are resistant to those particular pests or diseases: This is an important concept in organic gardening. Certain vegetables will resist blight, some types of peach trees are not susceptible to leaf curl, and so on. You want to fill your garden with the healthiest plants you can find so you'll have to spend less time trying to outwit unwanted visitors or harmful diseases. Interestingly, some insects don't seem to like healthy plants; they prefer the softer, sappier growth that characterizes plants raised on synthetic nitrogen fertilizers.

growing vegetables

As far as I am concerned, the heart of any organic garden is the vegetable plot. After all, despite the environmental benefits of organic gardening, it is the health benefits for you and your family that are the main reason for going organic.

Crop rotation is one tool for success when growing vegetables organically (see page 152), but first you have to decide what vegetables you want in your patch. If space is limited, I find it's better to grow things that are more expensive to buy or that aren't readily available, rather than devoting two-thirds of the space to organic potatoes. Delicious though they may be, they are cheap by comparison to organic artichokes and asparagus, and a lot easier to find.

If space isn't a concern, then plant as much as you like of all the root vegetables, the brassicas (broccoli, cauliflower, and cabbage), and everything else you know your family will enjoy. Inevitably you will have surpluses at some times of the year, but your own home-grown, home-frozen organic vegetables are infinitely better than any nonorganic produce, even if it's purchased fresh from your local market.

The vegetable varieties I mention below have all proved successful in my own garden, where the soil is heavy clay and the climate is mild. My traditional Victorian vegetable plot is in the open, where it gets maximum sunlight, but it is protected by a screen of holly hedge on one side.

Globe artichoke. You need plenty of space to grow globe artichokes, but they are so delicious and healthy for you (and expensive to buy) that it is worth devoting the space to grow them. Artichokes are easiest to grow in mild climates, so if you live in a northern climate, look for varieties that produce blooms in one season. (In California, as in England, you may be able to raise artichokes as perennials, but in most other places these delectable vegetables are grown as annuals.) 'Imperial Star' is one noteworthy cultivar that is easier to start from seed than most others. Nothing is more delicious than cutting off the tiny sideshoot buds and cooking them whole with pasta, as the Italians do, so be sure to give globe artichokes a try.

Jerusalem artichoke. Not to be confused with globe artichokes, this perennial is grown for its flowers and edible tubers. Be forewarned, they are highly prolific and will soon take over the garden if you are not careful. The tuber is

If you have plenty of space in your garden, grow brassicas and root crops as well as the more unusual—and expensive—vegetables.

difficult to peel but makes wonderful soup, or it can be eaten plain boiled, with melted butter and black pepper.

Asparagus. If you enjoy fresh asparagus but hate the high price, the effort to start an asparagus bed will be worth it. It's another perennial vegetable plant that is very difficult to start from seed, so bypass that route and opt for buying organic crowns. They are expensive initially, but having 6 to 8 weeks a year of abundant asparagus is an unimaginable treat. The bed does have to be weeded by hand, but you get the bonus of wonderful autumn ferns, which flower-arranging friends love. Once established, a good asparagus bed can last for as long as 20 years.

Fava beans. I always sow a row of fava beans in late autumn, and unless we have a very severe winter, they're producing well by early summer. If you live in a climate where winter temperatures dip below 10°F, you'll need to plant your beans in the spring. For the winter sowings I use 'Aguadulce', and in spring I plant 'Windsor'. Don't be greedy and wait for bean pods to get big in the hope that you will get masses of beans, or you'll be disappointed. Eat fava beans when they're small and tender—they're delicious and bursting with nutrients.

French beans, bush variety. Easy to grow and easy to pick, these round, slim beans are stringless if you pick them early. This is another very prolific vegetable, and if you stagger your sowings you will be eating them fresh from early spring through summer. They also freeze well. 'Maxibel' is a good variety to try—tender and tasty.

Runner beans. Freshly picked runner beans taste wonderful, but you have to pick them early. Scarlet runner beans are often grown for ornamental reasons, so if you miss picking the beans early, leave them on the plant and enjoy

Growing your own vegetables provides the perfect opportunity to experiment with unusual varieties such as bright green 'Romanesco' cauliflower (left) or rainbow chard (following pages) with its green, white, red, yellow, orange, and magenta stems and multicolored leaves.

their colorful show. Always leave enough unpicked beans to dry for next year's seeds.

Beets. Both the roots and leaves of beets are packed with nutrients. It's really worth growing this wonderful vegetable in your organic garden as it gets more and more difficult to buy fresh beets and is virtually impossible to find them with the leaves intact. The roots are delicious eaten as a vegetable, grated into a salad, made into soup, or juiced. The leaves can be cooked just like spinach. How different they are from the vinegar-soaked, precooked, canned versions sold in supermarkets. 'Detroit Dark Red' is a popular American variety. Beets should always be planted in succession. Choose several different varieties and eat them when they are golfball-sized. Baby beets boiled and served with a white sauce look and taste magnificent. Beets store well if kept in sand over the winter.

Chard. Chard grows like a weed once it is established, and the more you cut it the more it comes back. The multicolored variety produces red, yellow, and white stems and tinted leaves. Cook the leaves like spinach and the stems like asparagus. Serve with a little melted butter and a poached egg, and you'll be in nutritional and taste heaven.

Cabbage, broccoli, and cauliflower. Make sure you leave enough space to grow a wide selection of all the health-giving and cancer-protective members of the cabbage family. In many regions of the United States the summers are much harsher than they are where I live, so you may want to try different varieties than I grow. 'Early Jersey Wakefield' cabbage is good eating in early summer, and 'Roulette' is good for fall harvest. 'Red Acre' is perfect for coleslaw or any red cabbage dishes. If you want something different, try growing the Italian cauliflower 'Romanesco'. Cooked whole, the wonderful green color looks terrific in a serving dish. 'Snow Crown' is a cauliflower variety that produces quality heads whether it's sown for spring or fall cropping.

(continued on page 152)

The problem is that it's hard to stop once you start going through seed catalogs. You'll want lettuces, radishes, and certainly tomatoes. Try your hand at zucchini, even if it's only to have an endless supply of the flowers that are so delicious stuffed with ricotta cheese, and then deep-fried. Cucumbers, peppers, kohlrabi, leeks, onions—red, yellow, and spring—parsnips, turnips, peas, a dozen varieties of potatoes, and what about the pumpkins and squashes? Any good organic seed catalog will give you information about

(continued on page 156)

right: *Digging up your own potatoes is one of the most rewarding tasks in the organic garden.*
following pages: *Once you have tasted really fresh vegetables, you will want to grow a much wider variety, from parsnips and broccoli to white custard squashes and radicchio.*

CROP ROTATION

If you're really serious about growing vegetables, think about crop rotation, the time-honored key to organic growing. Vegetables from the same family are grown together and moved to a different plot each year to replenish lost nutrients and to prevent the build-up of pests and diseases common to that family. A 3-year plan is fine: You will need four beds for this rotation (including one bed for permanent crops).

Plot A can contain potatoes, tomatoes, eggplants, and peppers; celery, carrots, and parsnips; onions, shallots, leeks, and garlic; cucumbers, zucchini, summer squash, pumpkins, and melons.

Plot B can contain peas; French, runner, and fava beans; soybeans; peanuts; sweet corn; spinach; lettuce; okra; chicory; endive; and globe artichokes.

Plot C can contain cabbages, Chinese cabbage, brussels sprouts, cauliflower, broccoli, kale, rutabagas, turnips, radishes, and kohlrabi.

Plot D is for perennial crops: rhubarb, globe artichokes, Jerusalem artichokes, asparagus, and herbs. (Or, herbs can simply be planted among your flowers.)

Groups A, B, and C are planted in a different bed each year. Year 1, the pattern is A-B-C; year 2, B-C-A; and year 3, C-A-B.

GROWING FRUIT

If you want to grow soft fruit such as berries, you will need to allocate space for them—either as part of your vegetable plot or mixed in with your shrubs and flowers. You will need to protect fruit and berries with netting as they ripen; otherwise, the birds will get your fruit long before you do.

A lot of soft fruits ripen to perfection at the same time, so be prepared to freeze them, can them, or make them into jam, unless you want a lot of your hard work wasted.

I also recommend planting at least one apple tree—more if you have a large yard. Since apples are among the most heavily sprayed crops, this is one fruit that is really worth growing for the double benefit of chemical avoidance and good economic sense.

You'll find apple varieties to suit every space from a tiny backyard to a large country property. Multivariety trees grow from one stem and are miniaturized to fruit abundantly at a height of about 5 to 6 feet. Where possible, try to grow old varieties to preserve the biodiversity in your garden. The nursery where you buy your trees should be able to advise you on the best mix of varieties to plant together to ensure optimum pollination.

the wide choices you have. But don't be too ambitious if you're just starting out. You'll be hooked for life as soon as you have dug and cooked your first meal of new potatoes, or picked and eaten the earliest tender beans. There's always next year to add new crops.

the herb garden

I have a passion for herbs and, given the exorbitant price of a tiny packet of supermarket herbs (and organic herbs are even more exorbitant), I believe one of the most important features of any organic garden is the herb garden. You can grow a wide range of plants—both culinary and medicinal—and some that are never available in supermarkets or even at specialty stores. There are excellent suppliers of organic herbs who will advise you about the best varieties for your climate and soil conditions. No matter where you live, the raised bed concept is perfect for herbs because you can create growing conditions that are desired by most herbs. (See "The Benefits of Raised Beds" on page 136.)

Most of the strongly aromatic herbs are resistant to normal garden pests, and their pungent scents may actually help to protect other, more sensitive plants growing nearby from insects. With so many wonderful herbs, most of which are easy to grow, it can hard to decide where to start. Here are some recommendations if you're just starting out.

Basil. This annual herb is easy to grow from seed. 'Genovese' is the most sought-after variety for making Italian specialties such as pesto, but there are many other types to choose from. Some such as 'Red Rubin' have deep purple leaves; others like lemon, licorice, and cinnamon basils have unusual flavors.

Chives. Chives are so easy to grow that no garden should be without them. A perennial herb with grassy, onion-flavored leaves, the purple, pom-pom shaped flowers are edible, too. Snip fresh chives onto potatoes or salads, use the flowers in vinegars and salad dressings, and be sure to plant some chives under your roses to keep pests away.

Lavender. This herb, beloved for its aromatic qualities, lends a bit of Provence to every herb garden. A spiky plant with blue-gray leaves, lavender sends up whorls of purple flowers in midsummer. 'Hidcote' and 'Munstead' are two varieties that come through winters reliably as long as temperatures don't drop below -10°F.

Lemon balm. If you're looking for an herb that's easy to grow, you've found it! In fact, lemon balm is so easy to grow that once it gets established it tends to muscle its way into the rest of the garden. However, the lemon-scented leaves—which are so delightful in teas and potpourri—make it worth the trouble of trying to keep this vigorous grower in bounds. Try golden-leaved 'Aurea' to provide a bit of contrast against the dark green and blue-gray foliage commonly found in herb gardens.

Sage. A shrubby perennial herb with soft, pebbly leaves, sage looks equally at home in the herb garden or in an ornamental border. Sage offers both culinary and medicinal qualities, making it a perfect choice. It's intensely aromatic, with leaves available in a palette of colors from smoky blue-gray to mottled yellow-green to purple.

Thyme. Thyme comes in many shapes, sizes, and textures—from the tiny creepers that fill in between stepping-stones to the woolly types that spill out over the edges of the herb garden. Generally hardy in a wide range of zones, thyme is a perennial herb that prefers a sunny location.

Of course, my herb garden was a very ambitious project and I was lucky enough to have plenty of space to plant it. But however small your garden, patio, or window box, a selection of your favorite herbs will be not only an economic benefit but also a great way to attract bees and butterflies to your yard. Any of the herb gardening books listed in "Further Reading" on page 164 will give you detailed instructions on planting, growing, and propagating herbs.

shrub borders

Few people have the time to maintain huge borders of annual flowers that need to be dug up and replaced at least once or twice a year. I think that perennial borders can be almost as time-consuming, so I prefer to plant a shrub border with plants that need little attention. To reduce the need for weeding or continual mulching, plant groundcovers between your shrubs; they'll look nice and help block weeds. A mixture of groundcover roses, many of which are remarkably resistant to pests and diseases, and the small-leaved varieties of ivy can produce a stunning carpet of plants that needs no maintenance other than an occasional feeding with liquid organic fertilizer (see "Fertilizing" on page 137).

Choosing ornamental shrubs is a matter of individual taste, but the following suggestions may be useful as you plan your beds.

Japanese maple (*Acer palmatum*) is a wonderful miniature tree that grows to about 13 feet tall and equally as wide. Japanese maple provides glorious crimson autumn color. It prefers a partially shaded site.

Strawberry tree (*Arbutus unedo*) is a slow-growing evergreen with deep glossy leaves, a mass of flowers, and orange fruits. This sun lover can reach 15 to 25 feet and will grow in virtually any soil. It's hardy only in mild winter areas.

Butterfly bush (*Buddleia davidii*) has colorful flowers in shades of blues, lavenders, purples, pinks, magentas, and white that attract various butterfly species. Butterfly bush needs little care other than cutting back hard in early spring. It prefers a sunny spot in any well-drained soil.

California lilacs (*Ceanothus* spp.) are magnificent blue flowering shrubs. They require very little attention, although all varieties are more likely to thrive in a sheltered spot that gets plenty of sun.

Fatsias (*Fatsia* spp.) are often thought of as indoor plants, but if you live in a warm climate with mild winters and like the strong architectural leaves, this is a shrub that looks magnificent. You'll need to give it enough space in a sheltered spot in the shade; it will tolerate any reasonably fertile soil. It is incredibly easy to propagate from cuttings. Fatsias will reach 10 to 13 feet and bear wonderful cream flowers in autumn.

Witch hazel (*Hamamelis* spp.) produces a wonderful splash of color in the depths of winter. The bright yellow flowers of *H. mollis* (Chinese witch hazel) look startling against the bare branches, where they will appear from late winter to early spring. Cut a few stems and bring them indoors and enjoy the bonus of their delicate perfume. Witch hazel matures to 10 feet tall and equally as wide, but other than keeping it pruned to the available space, it needs little attention.

Rose of Sharon (*Hypericum calycinum*) is a wonderful groundcover smothered in bright yellow flowers from late spring to early autumn. It grows where most other things won't, especially under trees, and it's evergreen in sheltered conditions. It likes any soil, and needs no attention other than cutting back hard in the spring.

Bay laurel or sweet bay (*Laurus nobilis*) produces leaves that are essential in every kitchen. It is seldom grown as a garden shrub because it's hardy only in mild winter areas. Once established, it can reach 20 to 22 feet tall. It will grow in any fertile soil but does need to be sheltered from the wind. It is equally happy in shade or sun. If bay isn't hardy in your area, consider growing it as a container plant that you can move outside during summer and bring indoors in winter.

Mahonia (*Mahonia* spp.) is another of my favorites because of the wonderful architectural shape of the leaves and the different sizes of the varieties. From spreading, low growth to huge upright, reaching more than 7 feet tall, they make a beautiful graduated backdrop in a shrub border. They are evergreen with early yellow flowers, followed by purple-blue berries. Check with your nursery before buying, as some varieties are more cold hardy than others. Mahonia does well in all shady spots and in any type of soil.

Elders (*Sambucus* spp.) are not shrubs that normally come to mind as ornmental species, as many people consider them pests. Look for smaller garden species such as American elder (*S. canadensis*) or *S. nigra* 'Guincho Purple' that produce both flowers and berries with culinary uses. (Warning: Although the fruits are safe when cooked, all parts of the plant can cause severe discomfort when eaten, and contact with the leaves can irritate skin.) Elders will grow in most soils in full sun to partial shade.

looking to the future

Whether you have a few acres of garden or a small patio, a window box or just a few sunny windowsills, you can grow something edible and delicious. In my experience, when people start to grow one or two things for themselves, it becomes their launching pad into the whole world of organic living. Once you have an organic garden and begin making your own compost, you become much more aware of the natural cycles of growing plants and how they return to the soil to be reused as nutrients.

From gardening and eating organically, it is only a small step to thinking about the chemicals you put in your washing machine, the shampoo you put on your child's head, or the soap you use in the shower. There's no doubt in my mind that the microcosm of your own organic garden focuses the mind on the perils of the polluted macrocosm of the world in which we live. Those first steps on the surface of the moon may have been "one small step for man, one giant leap for mankind," but everyone who makes the first small step toward organic living is helping mankind take a giant step toward reducing greenhouse gases, deforestation, the wanton consumption of nonrenewable resources, and the risk of global warming, climate change, and chaos.

Every bottle you recycle, every drop of water you reuse, and every mile less you travel in your car is a small step toward a more hopeful future. The biggest step is bringing up our children to care for their planet. If we succeed, there is a chance that we will, by the combined efforts of millions, make that giant leap for mankind that allows us to pass on a greener and more pleasant world from generation to generation.

Adding plenty of compost to your soil and using organic mulches such as straw help nourish the soil. As a result, you won't have to resort to heavy doses of fertilizers for your garden.

••• sources

GOVERNMENT AGENCIES

Agency for Toxic Substance and Disease Registry (ATSDR)
1600 Clifton Road
Atlanta, GA 30333
Phone: (888) 422-8737
E-mail: ATSDRIC@cdc.gov
Web site: www.atsdr.cdc.gov

Environmental Protection Agency (EPA)
Ariel Rios Building
1200 Pennsylvania Avenue NW
Washington, DC 20460
Phone: (202) 260-2090
E-mail: public-access@epamail.epa.gov
Web site: www.epa.gov

U.S. Consumer Product Safety Commission
Washington, DC 20207-0001
Phone: (800) 638-2772
Web site: www.cpsc.gov

U.S. Department of Energy
1000 Independence Avenue SW
Washington, DC 20585
Phone: (800)-dial DOE (342-5363)
Fax: (202) 586- 4403
Web site: www.energy.gov

U.S. Department of Energy Fuel Ecomony Site
9300 Lee Highway
Fairfax, VA 22031
Phone: (800) 423-1363
E-mail: fueleconomy@ornl.gov
Web site: www.fueleconomy.gov/feg/index.htm
    Compares gas mileage, fuel costs, and emissions of new and used vehicles

Occupational Safety and Health Administration (OSHA)
Office of Public Affairs
200 Constitution Avenue, Room N3647
Washington, DC 20210
Phone: (202) 693-1999
Web site: www.osha.gov

U.S. Food and Drug Administration (FDA)
5600 Fishers Lane
Rockville, Maryland 20857
Phone: (888) 463-6332
Web site: www.fda.gov

CONSUMER ORGANIZATIONS

Alliance to End Childhood Lead Poisoning
227 Massachusetts Avenue NE, Suite 200
Washington, DC 20002
Phone: (202) 543-1147
Web site: www.aeclp.org

Center for Science in the Public Interest
1875 Connecticut Avenue, NW Suite 300
Washington, DC 20009
Phone: (202) 332-9110
Fax: (202) 265-4954
E-mail: cspi@cspinet.org
Web site: www.cspinet.org
    Nonprofit advocacy group that works to improve food safety and nutritional quality

Consumers Union
101 Truman Avenue
Yonkers, NY 10703–1057
Phone: (914) 378-2000
Web site: www.consumersunion.org
    Publisher of Consumer Reports *magazine*

Environmental Defense
(formerly Environmental Defense Fund)
257 Park Avenue South
New York, NY 10010
Phone: (800) 684-3322
Fax: (212) 505-2575
Web site: www.edf.org
    National nonprofit organization that links science, economics, and law to create innovative, equitable, and cost-effective solutions to urgent environmental problems

Environmental Working Group
1718 Connecticut Avenue NW, Suite 600
Washington, DC 20009
Web site: www.ewg.org
    Provides research on health and environmental issues

Greenpeace
702 H Street NW
Washington, DC 20001
Phone: (800) 326-0959
Web site: www.greenpeace.org
    International organization battling chemical pollution and environmental threats

Institute of Scrap Recycling Industries (ISRI)
1325 G Street NW, Suite 1000
Washington, DC 20005-3104
Phone: (202) 737-1770
Fax: (202) 626-0900
E-mail: isri@isri.org
Web site: www.isri.org

Beyond Pesticides
701 E Street SE #200
Washington, DC 20003

Phone: (202) 543-5450
Fax: (202) 543-4791
E-mail: info@beyondpesticides.org
Web site: www.beyondpesticides.org
National non-profit network committed to pesticide safety and the adoption of alternative pest management strategies to reduce or eliminate a dependency on toxic chemicals

Rainforest Action Network
221 Pine Street, Suite 500
San Francisco, CA 94104
Phone: (415) 398-4404
Fax: (415) 398-2732
Web site: www.ran.org
Works to protect the Earth's rain forests and their inhabitants through education, grassroots organizing, and non-violent direct action

Rocky Mountain Institute
1739 Snowmass Creek Road
Snowmass, CO 81654–9199
Phone: (970) 927-3851
E-mail: outreach@rmi.org
Web site: www.rmi.org
Fosters the efficient and restorative use of natural resources

United Nations Environment Program
Regional Office for North America
1707 H Street NW, Suite 300
Washington, DC 20006
Phone: (202) 785-0465
Fax: (202) 785-2096 or 785-4871
Web site: www.unep.org

World Resources Institute
10 G Street NE, Suite 800
Washington, DC 20002
Phone: (202) 729-7600
Fax: (202) 729-7610
E-mail: front@wri.org
Web site: www.wri.org
Provides information, ideas, and solutions to global environmental concerns

World Wide Fund for Nature
1250 Twenty-fourth Street NW
Washington, DC 20037
Phone: (800)-CALL-WFF (225-5993)
Web site: www.wwf.org
Dedicated to protecting the world's wildlife and wildlands

Zero Waste America (ZWA)
Phone: (215) 493-1070
Fax: (215) 493-2567
E-mail: lynnlandes@earthlink.net
Web site: www.zerowasteamerica.org
Promotes recycling of all materials back into nature or the marketplace in a manner that protects human health and the environment.

HEALTH ORGANIZATIONS

American Academy of Asthma, Allergy and Immunology
Phone: (800) 822-2762
Web site: www.aaaai.org

American Association of Oriental Medicine
433 Front Street
Catasauqua, PA 18032
Phone: (610) 266-1433
Fax: (610) 264-2768
Web site: www.aaom.org/states.html

American Association of Reflexologists (AAR)
4012 Rainbow Ste., K-PMB#585
Las Vegas, NV 89103-2059
E-mail: reflex@chazlo.com
Web site: www.reflexology-usa.org

American Herbalists Guild (AHG)
1931 Gaddis Road
Canton, GA 30115
Phone: (770) 751-6021
Fax: (770) 751-7472
E-mail: ahgoffice@earthlink.net
Web site: www.healthy.net/herbalists

American Naturopathic Association (ANA)
Web site: www.wnho.org/ana.htm

American Naturopathic Medical Association (ANMA)
PO Box 96273
Las Vegas, NV 89193
Phone: (702) 897-7053
Fax: (702) 897-7140
E-mail: webmaster@anma.com
Web site: www.anma.com

American Osteopathic Association
142 East Ontario Street
Chicago, IL 60611
Phone: (800) 621-1773
Fax: (312) 202-8200
E-mail: info@aoa-net.org
Web site: www.am-osteo-assn.org

American Osteopathic Healthcare Association
5550 Friendship Boulevard, Suite 300
Chevy Chase, MD 20815
Phone: (301) 968-2642
Fax: (301) 968-4195
Web site: www.aoha.org

American Society for the Alexander Technique (AmSAT)
Florence, MA 01062
Phone: (800) 473-0620
Web site: www.alexandertech.org

Council of Colleges of Acupuncture and Oriental Medicine
1424 16th St NW, Suite 501
Washington, DC 20036

National Acupuncture and Oriental Medicine Alliance
1833 North 105th Street
Seattle, WA 98133

National Center for Environmental Health Strategies (NCEHS)
1100 Rural Avenue
Voorhees, NJ 08043
Phone: (856) 429-5358
E-mail: ncehs@ncehs.org
Web site: www.ncehs.org

National Commission for the Certification of Acupuncturists
1424 16th Street NW, Suite 501
Washington, DC 20036

Physicians Committee for Responsible Nutrition
5100 Wisconsin Avenue NW, Suite 404
Washington, DC 20016
Phone: (202) 686-2210
Fax: (202) 686-2216
E-mail: pcrm@pcrm.org
Web site: www.pcrm.org

United States National Library of Medicine
8600 Rockville Pike
Bethesda, MD 20894
Web site: www.nlm.nih.gov

HOUSEHOLD AND BUILDING ORGANIZATIONS

American Forest and Paper Association (AF&PA)
1111 19th Street NW, Suite 800
Washington, DC 20036
Phone: (202) 463-2700
Fax: (202) 463- 2471
Web site: www.afandpa.org

The American Solar Energy Society (ASES)
2400 Central Avenue, Suite G-1
Boulder, CO 80301
Phone: (303) 443-3130
Fax: (303) 443-3212
E-mail: ases@ases.org
Web site: www.ases.org

American Wind Energy Association
122 C Street NW, Suite 380
Washington, DC 20001
Phone: (202) 383-2500
Fax: (202) 383-2505
E-mail: windmail@awea.org
Web site: www.awea.org

Center for Resourceful Building Technology
PO Box 100
Missoula, MT 59806
Phone: (406) 549-7678
Fax: (406) 549-4100
E-mail: crbt@ncat.org
Web site: www.crbt.org
Building materials from reused, salvaged, underutilized, or waste materials

Ecovillage Training Center, The Farm
560 Farm Road, PO Box 90
Summertown, TN 38483-0090
E-mail: ecovillage@thefarm.org
Web site: www.thefarm.org
A wide range of energy-saving and environmentally friendly technologies

Environmental Building News
122 Birge Street, Suite 30
Brattleboro, VT 05301
Phone: (802) 257-7300
Fax: (802) 257-7304
Web site: www.buildinggreen.com
Newsletter focused on environmentally responsible design and construction; provides source lists of products and services

EnviroSource.com, Inc.
1523 North Pascal Street, Suite 100
St. Paul, MN 55108-2328
Phone: (651) 645-0294
E-mail: info@envirosource.com
Web site: www.envirosource.com
An electronic enviro-mall that includes an e-store and links to environmental product suppliers, contractors, and organizations

Global Energy Marketplace
Web site: www.gem.crest.org
A gateway to sustainable energy information on the Web

The Green Design Network
Web site: www.greendesign.net
Searchable Internet database of more than 600 sites related to environmentally conscious design and construction

Sustainable Buildings Industry Council (SBIC)
1331 H Street NW, Suite 1000
Washington, DC 20005
Phone: (202) 628-7400
Fax: (202) 393-5043
Web site: www.sbicouncil.org
Provides guidelines, software, and general information about energy conservation measures, energy efficient equipment and appliances, daylighting, and sustainable architecture

Thermomax
5560 Sterrett Place, Suite 115
Columbia, Maryland 21044
Phone: (410) 997-0778
Fax: (410) 997-0779
E-mail: info@thermomax.com
Web site: www.thermomax.com
Solar energy systems

U.S. Green Building Council
1015 18th Street NW
Suite 805
Washington, DC 20036
Phone: (202) 828-7422
Fax: (202) 828-5110
Web site: www.usgbc.org
Promotes the adoption of green-building practices, technologies, policies, and standards

Yemm and Hart Green Materials
1417 Madison 308
Marquand, MO 63655-9153
Phone: (573) 783-5434
Fax: (573) 783-7544
Web site: www.yemmhart.com
Supplies information and samples of building materials, furniture, and other products made with recycled content

HEALTH AND BEAUTY PRODUCTS

As We Change
6255 Ferris Square, Suite F
San Diego, CA 92121-3232
Phone: (858) 456-8333
Fax: (858) 456-8340
Web site: www.aswechange.com
Variety of natural health products from reflexology clogs to botanical skin care

Aveda
4000 Pheasant Ridge Drive
Blaine, MN 55449
Phone: (800) 283-3224
Web site: www.aveda.com
Botanical hair care products and cosmetics

Gaiam, Inc.
360 Interlocken Boulevard, Suite 300
Broomfield, CO 80021-3440
Phone: (877) 989-6321
Fax: (800) 456-1139
Web site: www.gaiam.com
Organic food products and other items for natural living

The Helena Meyer Company
656 Main Avenue
Durango, CO 81301
Phone (970) 382-9409
Fax: (970) 382-2599
Web site: www.helenameyer.net
Organic skin care products and cosmetics

Weleda, Inc.
Customer Care
175 North Route 9W
Congers, NY 10920
Phone: 800-241-1030
Web site: www.usa.weleda.com
Organic and biodynamic personal care products; homeopathic medicines

CHILDREN'S PRODUCTS

Babyworks
11725 NW West Road
Portland, OR 97229
Phone: (800) 422-2910
Web site: www.babyworks.com
Cotton and wool diapers, diaper covers, wipes, untreated blankets, natural fiber dolls

Children's Health Environmental Coalition (CHEC)
PO Box 1540
Princeton, NJ 08542
Phone: (609) 252-1915
Fax: (609) 252-1536
E-mail: chec@checnet.org
Web site: www.checnet.org
Nonprofit research organization that examines causes of childhood cancers

Earthlings
c/o Gaiam International
321 Hampton Drive
Venice, CA 90291
Phone: (877) 737-8648
Organic cotton sheets, blankets, mattresses, clothing, diapers, bath towels, stuffed animals, cribs, cotton slings, toys

Ecobaby
1475 North Cuyamaca
El Cajon, CA 92020
Phone: (888) 596-7450
Web site: www.ecobaby.com
Furniture; organic cotton bedding, bath towels, toys and clothing; disposable diapers

Eco-wise Environmental Products
110 West Elizabeth Street
Austin, TX 78704
Phone: (512) 326-4474
Web site: www.ecowise.com
Organic cotton diapers, pads, covers; nursing pads; organic cotton clothing, bedding, mattresses, and baby slings; organic baby food

Natural Baby Company
7835 Freedom Avenue NW
North Canton, OH 44720-6907
Phone: (800) 388-2229
Furniture, cotton and wool blankets, mattress pads, diapers, nursing pads, bras, and more

HOME ACCESSORIES

Breathefree.com, Inc.
12611 Hidden Creek Way, Suite E
Cerritos, CA 90703
Phone: (888) 434-8313
Web site: www.breathefree.com
HEPA filter vacuums, freestanding humidi-fiers, humidifiers that attach to furnaces, electronic air cleaners with HEPA filters

Center for Neighborhood Technology
2125 W. North Avenue
Chicago, IL 60647
Phone: (773) 278-4800
E-mail: info@cnt.org
Web site: www.cnt.org/wetcleaning/
Information about less-toxic alternatives for dry cleaning clothes

DesignTex
Phone: (800) 221-1540
Web site: www.dtex.com
Fabric and textile manufacturer

Environmental Home Center
1724 Fourth Avenue S
Seattle, WA 98134
Phone: (206) 682-7332 or
　　　　(800) 281-9785
Fax: (206) 682-8275
Web site: www.enviresource.com

Foxfibre
PO Box 66
Wickenburg, AZ 85358
Phone: (520) 684-7199
Web site: www.foxfibre.com
Naturally colored organic cotton products

The Green Culture
PO Box 1684
Laguna Beach, CA 92652
Phone: (800) 233-8438
Web site: www.greenculture.com
Nontoxic pest and rodent control

Harmony
360 Interlocken Boulevard
Broomfield, CO 80021
Phone: (800) 456-1177
Web site: www.gaiam.com
Cleaning products, anti-allergy sprays and powders, HEPA air filters and vacuums, fans

Healthy Home Center
1403-A Cleveland Street
Clearwater, FL 33755
Phone: (800) 583-9523
Web site: www.healthyhome.com
Alternative rug shampoos, paint removers without methylene chloride

Interlock Paving Systems, Inc.
802 West Pembroke Avenue
Hampton, VA 23699
Phone: (800) 572-3189
Fax: (757) 723-8895
E-mail info@interlockonline.com
Website: www.interlockonline.com/
environ.html
Manufacturers of permeable, interlocking driveway stones

Patagonia
8550 White Fir Street
PO Box 32050
Reno, NV 89533-2050
Phone: (800) 638-6464
E-mail: customer_service@patagonia.com
Web site: www.patagonia.com
Supplier of organic cotton garments and fleece garments made from recycled plastic bottles; donates 1 percent of sales to environmental causes

Real Goods Trading Company
200 Clara Street
Ukiah, CA 95482
Phone: (800) 762-7325
Web site: www.realgoods.com
Mattress covers, organic cotton mattresses and pillows, untreated cotton towels and curtains, rugs, HEPA air purifiers

Seventh Generation
One Mill Street, Box A26
Burlington, VT 05401-1530
Phone: (802) 658-3773
Fax: (802) 658-1771
Web site: www.seventhgen.com
Supplier of domestic and building products; database on chemicals and pollution

GARDENING

A.M. Leonard, Inc.
241 Fox Drive, P.O. Box 816
Piqua, OH 45356-0816
Phone: (800) 543-8955
Fax: (800) 433-0633
E-mail: info@amleo.com
Web site: www.amleo.com
Large selection of tools

W. Atlee Burpee
300 Park Avenue
Warminster, PA 18974
Phone: (800) 888-1447
Fax: (215) 674-4170
E-mail: burpeecs@surfnetwork.net
Web site: www.burpee.com
Seeds and plants of annuals, perennials, vegetables and herbs

The Cook's Garden
PO Box 535
Londonderry, VT 05148
Phone: (800) 457-9703
Fax: (800) 457-9705
E-mail: gardener@cooksgarden.com
Web site: www.cooksgarden.com
Seeds and supplies for the kitchen gardener

Forestfarm
990 Tetherow Road
Williams, OR 97544-9599
Phone: (541) 846-7269
Fax: (541) 846-6963
Web site: www.forestfarm.com
Ornamental plants including many American native varieties

Gardens Alive!
5100 Schenley Place
Lawrenceburg, IN 47025
Phone: (812) 537-8651
Fax: (812) 537-5108
E-mail: gardenhelp@gardensalive.com
Web site: www.gardens-alive.com
Organic fertilizers and pest controls, corn gluten meal for weed control; also natural pet care products

Gardener's Supply Company
128 Intervale Road
Burlington, VT 05401
Phone: (888) 833-1412
Fax: (800) 551-6712
E-mail: info@gardeners.com
Web site: www.gardeners.com
Organic fertilizers and pest control; also tools, seed-starting supplies and home products

Johnny's Selected Seeds
Foss Hill Road
Albion, ME 04910
Phone: (207) 437-4357
Fax: (800) 437-4290
E-mail: johnnys@johnnyseeds.com
Web site: www.johnnyseeds.com
Vegetable, herb and flowers seeds; also tools, organic fertilizers and pest control products

Niche Gardens
1111 Dawson Road
Chapel Hill, NC 27516
Phone: (919)967-0078
Email: staff@nichegdn.com
Web site: www.nichegdn.com
Nursery-propagated wildflowers and perennials

Peaceful Valley Farm Supply
PO Box 2209
Grass Valley, CA 95945
Phone: (888) 784-1722
Fax: (530) 272-4794
E-mail: contact@groworganic.com
Web site: www.groworganic.com
*Tools, seeds, fertilizers, pest controls, and
natural pet care products*

Pinetree Garden Seeds
PO Box 300
New Gloucester, ME 04260
Phone: (207) 926-3400
Fax: (888) 527-3337
E-mail: superseeds@worldnet.att.net
Web site: www.superseeds.com
*Specializes in small packets of vegetable, herb
and flower seeds at reduced prices*

Prairie Nursery
PO Box 306
Westfield, WI 53964
Phone: (800) 476-9453
Fax: (608) 296-2741
E-mail: cs@prairienursery.com
Web site: www.prairienursery.com
*Native prairie, wetland and woodland
wildflowers, grasses and sedges for low-
maintenance gardens and meadows*

Smith and Hawken
PO Box 6900
Florence, KY 41022-6900
Phone: (800) 940-1170
Fax: (606) 727-1166
E-mail: smithandhawkencustomerservice
@discovery.com
Web site: www.smith-hawken.com
Garden tools and related products

Territorial Seed Co.
PO Box 157
Cottage Grove, OR 97424
Phone: (541) 942-9547
Fax: (888) 657-3131
E-mail: tertrl@srvl.vsite.com
Web site: www.territorial-seed.com
*Seed selected for short seasons and cool
climates*

Wildginger Woodlands
PO Box 1091
Webster, NY 14580
Northeastern wildflowers and ferns

... further reading

Balfour, Lady Eve. *The Living Soil.* London: Faber & Faber, 1943.

Berthold-Bond, Annie. *Better Basics for the Home.* New York: Three Rivers Press 1999.

Berthold-Bond, Annie, and Mothers & Others for a Livable Planet. *Green Kitchen Handbook.* New York: Harper Collins Books, 1997.

Bower, Lynn Marie. Creating a Healthy Household: The Ultimate Guide for Healthier, Safer, Less-Toxic Living. Bloomington, IN: The Healthy House Institute, 2000.

Bradley, Fern Marshall, and Barbara Ellis, eds. *Rodale's All-New Encyclopedia of Organic Gardening.* Emmaus, PA: Rodale, Inc., 1992.

Bradley, Fern Marshall, ed. *Rodale's Chemical-Free Yard and Garden.* Emmaus, PA: Rodale, Inc., 1991.

Brower, Michael, and Warren Leon. *The Consumer's Guide to Effective Environmental Choices: Practical Advice from the Union of Concerned Scientists.* New York: Three Rivers Press 1999.

Carson, Rachel. *Silent Spring.* New York: Houghton Mifflin, 1962; Penguin, 1999.

Cummins, Ronnie, and Ben Lilliston. *Genetically Engineered Food: A Self-Defense Guide for Consumers.* New York: Marlowe & Company, 2000.

Dadd-Redalia, Debra. *Sustaining the Earth; Choosing Consumer Products That Are Safe for You, Your Family, and the Earth.* New York: Hearst Books, 1994.

Ellis, Barbara W., and Fern Marshall Bradley. *The Organic Gardener's Handbook of Natural Insect and Disease Control.* Emmaus, PA: Rodale, Inc., 1996.

Needleman, Herbert L. MD, and Philip J. Landrigan, MD. *Raising Children Toxic Free.* New York: Farrah, Straus, and Giroux, 1994.

Ogden, Shepherd. *Step by Step Organic Vegetable Gardening: The Gardening Classic Revised and Updated.* New York: Harper-Collins, 1992.

Olkowski, William, et al. *The Gardener's Guide to Common-Sense Pest Control.* Newtown, CT: The Taunton Press, 1995.

Pennybacker, Mindy, and Aisha Ikramuddin. *Mothers and Others for a Livable Planet: Guide to Natural Baby Care.* New York: John Wiley & Sons, Inc. 1999.

Schultz, Warren. *The Organic Suburbanite: An Environmentally Friendly Way to Live the American Dream.* Emmaus, PA: Rodale, Inc., 2001

Shapiro, Howard-Yana, and John Harrisson. *Gardening for the Future of the Earth.* New York, NY: Bantam Books, 2000.

Smith, Miranda. *Your Backyard Herb Garden: A Gardener's Guide to Growing Over 50 Herbs Plus How To Use Them In Cooking, Crafts, Companion Planting and More.* Emmaus, PA: Rodale, Inc. 1996.

Stein, Sara. *Noah's Garden: Restoring the Ecology of Our Own Back Yards.* New York: Houghton Mifflin Company, 1993.

Steinman, David. *The Safe Shopper's Bible: A Consumer's Guide to Nontoxic Household Products, Cosmetics and Food.* New York, NY: Macmillan, 1995.

van Straten, Michael. *Guarana—The Energy Seeds and Herbs of the Amazon Rain Forest.* Safffron Walden: C. W. Daniel, 1994.

... index

••• acknowledgments

Michael van Straten

Patience, they say, is a virtue and it's one that has been hugely evident in all those concerned with the publication of this book, with the possible exception of myself. Frances Lincoln herself, Ginny Surtees, Serena Dilnot, and Fiona Robertson have all shown great patience, tolerance, and perseverance during the somewhat prolonged gestation of this book. I'd like to thank them all for their faith in the ultimate natural birth of this volume. The photographs by David Loftus are exquisite and encapsulate the true importance and meaning of organic living. I also thank my secretary, Janet Betley, for yet more gallons of midnight oil and separation from her family.

David Loftus

Thank to *Gardens Illustrated*, *Waitrose Food Illustrated* @ John Brown Publishing, Chelsea Physic Garden, Susie Theodorou, Tara Fisher, David Davies of Futurebrand, Mark Orme and David Matzdorf, Bob and Liz Callender, Karen Millen, and Sue and Allan Fox: Rodale Inc. jacket: styled by David Davies; p.3: Karen Miller/designer; p.8: Bob and Liz Callender/artists; p.26: photo Tara Fisher/*Waitrose Food Illustrated*; p.29 lower left and right: Tara Fisher/*Food Illustrated*; p.29 top left & right: Sue and Allan Fox, owners of Bringalbit, Melbourne; p.30: Paros Loftus, age 3; p.48: Andy Harris's picnic; p.66: Beeker; p.70: Wall model; p.77: bottom right Debbie Loftus; p.84: Wall model; p.86: Estelle @ Nevs; p.100: David Davies/designer; p.107: Mark Orme/architect; p.108/9 Matzdorf House/architect John Broome and Tim Crosskey of Architype 2000; p.115: model Cosima; p.116: Matzdorf House; p.117: Karen Millen/designer; p.118/119: Mark Orme/architect; p.120: Matzdorf House; p.121: Mark Orme/architect; p.122: Mark Orme/architect; p.123: Bringalbit, Australia; p.125: Mark Orme/architect; p.127: Matzdorf House

••• credits

Rodale Inc.
Executive Editor: Kathleen DeVanna Fish
Managing Editor: Fern Marshall Bradley
Executive Creative Director: Christin Gangi
Art Director: Patricia Field
Editor: Karen Costello Soltys
Researcher: Diana Erney
Copy Manager: Nancy N. Bailey
Copy Editors: Sarah Sacks Dunn, Jennifer M. Blackwell, Linda Brunner
Manufacturing Coordinator: Jodi Schaffer